DISCOVER YOUR SPIRITUAL STRENGTHS

AND FIND HEALTH, HEALING & HAPPINESS

Learn a new method to …

- **Become the true you … your authentic self**

- **Heal your illness … whatever it may be**

- **Maximize your spiritual strengths … divine grace**

- **Harness your full personality power**

- **Achieve inner peace and spiritual vitality**

Richard P. Johnson, Ph.D.

ISBN 978-0-9743623-4-2

10 9 8 7 6 5 4 3   2   1

Cover design by Megan Irwin

Printed in the United States of America

Contents

Introduction

This book is about how to use your God-given personality strengths as your primary healing and spiritual deepening tool. It's about how to dedicate your personality to the task of healing; it's about finding the secret of healing, and discovering the keys that unlock the mystery of the real you. It's about discovering the true, genuine, no-mask 'you.'

The overall goal of this book is to help you ...

Discover your individual, unique, and special spiritual formula for healing whatever kind of pain or brokenness you may be experiencing right now.

To achieve this overarching goal this book brings you on a tour of your personality, a grand adventure that will change the way you see yourself and your illness or brokenness. This book helps you address other tasks that seem rather grandiose as I survey them now, yet there's a simplicity in their grandness that speaks with authority. These tasks stop me in wonder even now; they captivate me.

This book will help you ...

1. Discover the authentic *you*, the six spiritual strengths that power your personality and propel you toward healing and a deeper spiritual life.

2. Uncover the unique regressive forces (there are 12 of them) that block you from expressing the true *you*, and finding healing and peace.

3. Learn some practical ways of expressing your specialness so that you can grow closer to the real *you*, offer your personal strengths to others more fully, and cement healing to your personality.

4. Align your personality by forging a more comfortable fit between the "you" that you show the world, and the authentic *you*.

5. Discover new and deeper connections with "the divine presence" within you.

6. Develop a new sense of personal meaning, utility, and significance in your world.

7. Become equipped to walk shoulder-to-shoulder with others as a healing companion or Certified Spiritual Strengths Healing Coach.

The magic of this book is that it guides you to the spiritual core of your personality and coaches you toward discovering your true personality power.

Take The Spiritual Strengths Finder

Let me ask you right now to go ahead and take the Spiritual Strengths Finder. This is a 120 item educational and inspirational instrument that will give you a personal profile of your unique spiritual strengths. You take the Spiritual Strengths Finder right on the Internet; simply go to www.healyourillness.com and follow the directions there.

The Spiritual Strengths Finder gives you a 20-page personalized overview of your six premier spiritual strengths, as well as the personality shadows and compulsions that stand as dark sentinels on either side of your spiritual strengths. The information you receive about your personality will enrich you and allow you to get the most out of this book, but most of all, your results give you a formula for moving beyond suffering.

Your spiritual strengths are the internal fortitude or energy that shapes your personality in everything you do. Just knowing these six strengths gives a boost to your self-esteem, and a distinct advantage in improving every aspect of your life. The shadows and compulsions of each of your spiritual strengths are the regressive forces that can cause you to repeatedly trip over the same emotional, psychological and spiritual stumbling blocks that can sometimes make your life journey seem like a hard pull. This book, together with the Spiritual Strengths Finder, give you a way to break free of the self-destructive chains that impede your progress toward healing and personal fulfillment.

As a practicing professional counselor for more than 25 years, I have seen first-hand the damage caused by personality blocks. I have also stood witness to the miracle of how some persons are able to capture and use God's grace and un-block their personality finding release in ways well beyond the personality theories I've studied. Driven by these revelations, I ventured into what became a long-term qualitative research project, conducted in a large teaching hospital. The study brought me to 'places' of wonder, and gave me new insight into how our individual personality works.

Since writing the first book that grew out of this study, (_Body, Mind, Spirit_) I have taught my research findings to thousands of persons, professionals and laypersons alike. I have continuously added to, learned more about, and refined the results of this study until today when they have reached a new, and more practical level, and are ready for a wider public forum. This 'advanced and evolving discovery' serves now as the super-structure of an entirely new understanding of personality.

The book is divided into three parts. Part one, _The Mechanics of Your Personality_, gives you an exciting new view of personality, and a new perspective on how you can begin to optimize your personality. Chapter one describes how your personality works. Chapter two offers a lively narrative description of the research that spawned this book. Chapter three covers the captivating relationship between spiritual strengths and God's universal energy. Finally, chapter four presents a deeper explanation of spiritual strengths, personality shadows, and character compulsions.

Part two of the book, _Your Personality Comes to Life_, contains twelve chapters. There are two chapters devoted to each of the six functions of the personality. The first of these two chapters thoroughly describes that particular personality function, while the second gives definitions of each the spiritual strengths in that function together with short stories that give life to the strengths, shadows, and compulsions.

Part three, _The Dynamics of Your Personality_, puts everything together. It offers specific ways that this new perspective, and the new personal information that you gleaned from your Spiritual Strengths Finder results can be folded together so you can harness your spiritual strengths for a better life. In the three chapters of part three you'll discover how the many components of your personality can work together rather than in contention. You'll learn specific strategies to make your personality more hardy, more mentally, emotionally, and spiritually solid. You'll uncover how to use your personality to heal what may be fragmented in your life. Finally, you'll learn how you can help others by using the information in this book.

I see this book as the keystone of all my books. This is the one at the center, supporting the rest, giving completion to all the others. This book comes from a deeper place inside me. After years of thought, study, and research I feel more like a scribe taking dictation from God, rather than its author.

I like to think of myself as standing with you as you learn to use your personality for healing and optimal living. I'd like to see your face as you discover the essential wonder and divinity-reflection of your personality. I'd like to share your awe and advancing delight as you successively uncover the spiritual depth of your central 'life processor,' your personality. I'd like to be with you as you 'grow' your relationship with the God-given power and might within you, as you learn how to harness it, and as you use it to bring a new level of living and loving into your life. While I can't be physically with you, rest assured, I'm spiritually with you.

R. P. Johnson

Part One

The Mechanics of Your Personality: the Spiritual Wellspring of Healing

Healing means placing your primary trust in the core spiritual strengths that lay at the center of the real you. As you do, you gradually transcend the old and find rebirth in a new spirit; you discover the true power of your personality. You learn to place yourself at the disposal of that which is most real about you, the "packet" of divinity that gives you life.

> *Healing means shifting away from the center that you thought was you, and rebalancing on a new center of gravity, a spiritual center, an interior place where the true you resides.*

Your personality is the wellspring of all that you believe you are and all that you show to others. You are known to yourself and to others only by how you use your personality; use it well and you'll come to know yourself and find healing from whatever brokenness or illness that may have befallen you, use it poorly and you'll remain confused and ill equipped to deal with life's challenges. Your personality expresses the uniqueness of you among all others. It's the vehicle that allows you to communicate what's most important about you ... your true heart's desire.

Yet most of us are blithely ignorant of the intricacies of our personalities. We ask ourselves, *"What's my personality all about?" "Where or what is the source of my personality?"* We all ask these questions, sometimes consciously and most times not. We constantly strive to get a firmer grasp of this intangible executive of our lives called personality; sadly many of us never do.

In Part One of this book you'll learn how your personality is constructed and what it's supposed to do for you. This alone will give you advanced confidence in how you might be able to find healing of whatever "ails" you. In the process you'll discover a bonus, how to make your personality sparkle. In later chapters you'll fine-focus on your specific personality, and in so doing, discover new light, new life, and new healing.

Chapter One

Is the *You* that You Show the World Your Authentic Personality?

Do you sometimes have the feeling that the "you" that you are to the world may not be the *you* that you truly are? Even worse, have you recognized that you can be many different "yous" depending on whom you're with and where you are? If you've ever asked yourself these questions, you're not alone; you've simply encountered the mystery of your interior life, the single most perplexing question that bedevils us all ... "Who's the real me?" This book will give you an answer to this question.

There are no two identical personalities!

The population of the world is getting close to seven billion, yet there are no two identical personalities among all these people. In fact, in the entire history of humankind there has never been another personality just like yours. Even more incredibly, there never will be another! Your personality is unique, distinct, one-of-a-kind, unmistakable, and a never-to-be duplicated entity. Your real personality is a singular reflection of God. Your fundamental life 'job,' and your path to happiness, is to reflect this bestowal of divinity in and through yourself, and as you do, you find healing.

So, what is a personality, and why do you need such a special one? A personality is the sum total of your individual traits all admixed in ways both known and unknown, folded one on and into another, stirred by time and relationship, education and experience, as well as all of your emotional, psychological, attitudinal, and spiritual specialness, that together distinguish you as you. Everything that is your 'being' is somehow mixed together into this unique creation we call personality. Of course this begs another question, "What is your being?" This question is a hard one, but I hope that the answer will unfold for you in our journey through these pages. Perhaps a more practical question right now is, "Why have a personality?" or "What is the function of my personality? Before we can answer this question, we need to make an assertion. What do you think of this statement?

Every personality is specially gifted.

Another way to say this is that every person has unique gifts, or strengths. But, how are we gifted ... what are our gifts or strengths? Innately we seem to know that we are gifted; most every person will say, "Yes, I'm gifted." But when they try to enumerate their own gifts, they become quite stymied. Why do we have such a hard time answering what appears such a simple question? We know we have gifts, but what are they?

We believe that we are unique, one-of-a-kind creatures, yet most of us are quite unaware of how this uniqueness gets translated into our everyday reality. Here then, is the purpose, the singular task of your personality:

Your personality communicates the uniqueness of you.

Your personality never stops communicating the uniqueness of you, never stops expressing your specialness ... your gifts ... your strengths. Everything about you is processed through and expressed by, your personality, every word, gesture, action, *faux pas,* insinuation, attitude, insight, outlook, thought, feeling, and choice is a product of your personality. The total specialness of you is made by, and filtered through, the various screens or filters of your personality. But how does your personality accomplish all of this? The overall purpose of your personality, communicating the uniqueness of you, is carried out by these six functions of your personality.

1. Your *Believing* function

2. Your *Perceiving* function

3. Your *Thinking* function

4. Your *Feeling* function

5. Your *Deciding* function, and

6. Your *Acting* function

1) Your *Believing* function:
What you think your life should be like

The first function of your personality is your believing function.

Together your beliefs make-up what is called your *belief core*, the sum total of your 'truth.' Your beliefs include your values and your attitudes, as well as your assumptions about life, and whatever principles you live by. Here is the depository of all that you hold to be true about everything; it's your conception of the world according to you. How many beliefs your personality believing function contains is uncountable, but for sure it's a lot! You have beliefs about floors and ceilings, about sunshine and rain, about colors, and trees, and rocks, and buildings. You have beliefs about family and friends, industry and work, fun and drudgery, food and drink, relaxation and money. On a different plane, you have beliefs about yourself, your self-esteem, your mood, your purpose, your love or loves, your sense of adequacy or not, and a whole lot more. You have beliefs about sickness and illness, health and pain. You have beliefs about faith, higher power, cosmic communion, divinity, and love.

Your beliefs are like the data operating system in your computer. If you use *Microsoft* products on your computer, you use an operating system called "*Windows*." Windows is the 'truth' for that computer. If you didn't have Windows installed, you couldn't use any of the Microsoft programs because your computer wouldn't know how to read them. Your beliefs are like that; you wouldn't be able to 'read' the world around you, or inside you for that matter, if you didn't first have an 'operating system' called your belief core. Freudian psychology, or psychodynamic psychotherapy, approaches the personality primarily from the believing function.

2) Your *Perceiving* function:
Where you place your focus

The world is constantly bombarding you with data. This input comes from your surroundings, your total internal and external environments as they exist in place and time. When you look out your personality window, you're confronted with lots of stimuli. You 'pick-up' these stimuli and convert them, or perceive them as data with your senses, what you can see, taste, hear, touch, and smell. You also have other sensory pick-up devices; take intuition for instance. When two people meet a third person and have a short interchange, each walks away with certain sensations they have perceived from one another. What makes the first person focus on what the third person is wearing, while the second person focuses on, or perceives, the third person's feelings? Psychologists tell us that we only pick-up a small percentage of the data available to us. What makes us focus on some things and reject, or pass over others? We tend to focus mostly on two categories of data; those that we are familiar and agree with, and those that we don't. Critics focus on the later, while lovers, it's said focus on the former. Gestalt therapy, championed by the psychologist Fritz Perls, approaches the personality from the perceiving function.

3) Your *Thinking* function:
The meaning you make from your perceptions

How often do you think? How often do you 'make meaning' from all those data that are bombarding you continuously? Thoughts are your cognitions, the internal evaluations or assessments you make about the data you perceive. If you didn't have thoughts you couldn't make any sense of the calliope of data that is constantly buzzing, whining, screaming, and demanding to be noticed. The world continues to get more and more effective (not necessarily better) at increasing the volume of data and the speed at which it 'comes at you.' It's your thoughts that give order to all of this apparent confusion.

The psychotherapeutic modality known as cognitive therapy approaches the personality from the thinking function. A cognitive therapist is primarily interested in how you interpret your world, your actions and thoughts, and how you interpret the actions and thought of those around you. Your thoughts actually create your world, your reality; whatever you 'think' is accepted by the psyche as though it were true, even if it isn't. So a cognitive therapist draws out and evaluates your thoughts, illuminates them, and tries to determine their accuracy. Cognitive therapy's underlying assumption is the more accurate your thinking, the more your life will be your own. Cognitive therapy, originated by Aaron Beck, M.D., and popularized by David Burns, M.D., approaches the personality through the thinking function.

4) Your *Feeling* function:
The automatic emotions that flow from your thoughts

Feelings are the affective consequence of the thoughts you give yourself. If your thoughts are continuously negative, critical, offensive, or judging, then your immediate emotional reactions, or feelings, will be the same. Your feelings are a perfect reflection of your thinking, whatever meaning you make from the data that you allow into your cognitive system, will automatically determine your feelings. For example, if you look outside and say, "It's a nice day," then your feelings will turn slightly toward the positive, personally enabling side of the spectrum. If, on the other hand, you say, "It's a lousy day," then your feelings will swing toward the negative or paralyzing side of the spectrum. The day hasn't changed at all, but your perception of it, and especially the thoughts you entertain about it, generates the feelings you experience within yourself. Your thinking produces the internal terrain of your feelings. The so-called 'client centered', or 'Rogerian' therapeutic modality approaches your personality from your feelings function.

5) Your *Deciding* function:
The choices you make about your life based on your feelings

It's been said that your life is made up of decisions, decisions, and more decisions. The fact is that you must make decisions; when and if you stop making decisions your forward growth movement stops. Decisions are said to originate from your free will, yet there are many people who forfeit their free will to other forces or persons outside themselves. Such people hand the reigns of their lives over to someone else; they become dependent on these 'others' to run their lives. So afraid of making a mistake, such persons constantly survey the horizon of their lives looking for someone or something to take over their free will. Naturally they are not at all aware of their forfeiting pattern, nor are they aware of the consequences of giving their lives over to another. So-called 'Reality Therapy,' or what is now called 'Choice Therapy,' championed by William Glaser, approaches the personality through the deciding function.

6) Your *Acting* function:
Your behavior ...what you actually do!

After you, consciously or not, travel through the other five functions of your personality; you finally arrive at the last one, your acting function. Here in the acting function is where you put together all your 'work' from your previous five personality functions and form your unique behavior; you act in reality ... you 'do' something. The product of this function is what the world sees of you. The world doesn't take note of your believing, perceiving, thinking, feeling, and deciding 'work, since the world can't see these. It can only see your behavior ... what you actually do. Your actions are the end point, the culmination of all interior 'work' in the other five functions. Christian scripture connotes this fact well when it asserts, "You will know them by their fruits (actions)." The 'Behaviorist' psychotherapeutic modality approaches the personality through the acting function.

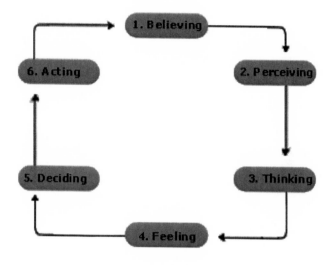

The six functions of the personality don't act independently of one another, they act in succession; they flow from one to another. This graphic portrays the sequential nature of your personality. Note the arrow that begins at the first function, believing, and swings through all six of the functions. The product or 'work' of one function is transmitted to the next function. The work of your personality is sequential. One personality function provides the raw material for the next function; this next function can only work well to the degree that the 'material' it receives from the previous function is clear, accurate, and complete. For example, if a person is weak in her/his feelings function, then the 'material' that is sent out by the feelings function to the deciding function will be faulty or lacking. The deciding function now works at a disadvantage because its raw material is insufficient for it to perform well. Consequently the work of the deciding function will likewise be faulty, resulting in a choice that is to some degree distorted. In turn, this distorted choice is forwarded to the acting function, leading to behavior that is at least equally distorted unless something or someone intervenes before hand.

You'll find a lot more about your personality functions in later chapters, however, let's just say that these six are always at work processing, collating, mixing, matching, comparing, evaluating, responding to, reacting from, and doing, doing, doing. Yet, all that they do has only one purpose … communicating the real you, warts and all, to the world. The better your personality accomplishes this one purpose, the happier, healthier, and whole-er you'll become. When you're accurately expressing your genuine giftedness, your authentic *you*, you not only feel better, work better, love better, relate better, like yourself better, play better, and communicate better, beyond all of this, you'll actually <u>be</u> better, because you are more *you*. You will have found healing.

Your Persona

Dr. Karl Jung coined a term to describe the outward 'you' that you show the world, he called it your *persona,* or mask. You, and all of us, construct an overall, or general persona that you show most of the time in your daily life. But you modify your persona, you 'morph' it into entirely different variations as you move from one life situation to another. For example, when you meet someone for the first time, you naturally want to 'put your best foot forward,' so you put on a persona that says, "I'm a good, understanding, polite, generous, caring, and respectful person." The next day at work you may put on a persona that says something like, "I'm efficient, effective, smart, savvy, and a can-do person." The next day when you're with friends your persona says things like, "I'm one of you." "I'm a good group member." "I'm committed to this group." You may even speak differently to accommodate each of these personas; you choose different words, different voice inflections, spacing, speed, and accent of speech as parts of your different personas. You may even adopt a different posture, clothes, attitudes, perspectives, etc. to support your various personas.

These personas are quite functional, giving you a flexibility of behavior that lets you adapt to lots of situations and people. The trouble is that you might come to believe that the personas you construct are the real, genuine 'you' when actually they're only facsimiles of the real 'you.' Your various personas hide the parts of you that you don't care to show at that time and place. The first impression "good guy/gal" image or persona is you of course, but only a small part of you ... there's a lot more of you that you choose not to show. You can never show the fullness of the real 'you' at any one time, so you pick and choose among all the parts of you and construct a persona that fits the situation that best meets your needs as you see them at that time and place. Over time, you develop several personas that become your standard ones; you may have a work persona, a church persona, a friend persona, you may have another persona you use when out shopping, playing, or just 'hanging out.' You may even have a persona you put on with those who know you the best. As these personas become standardized, they become your individuality – the unique 'you' the world believes you are. Yet you're much more than the succession of masks or personas you use to project parts of yourself.

Most of us are afraid to put our personas aside because we're not sure what we might show; we're afraid of the dark inside us. The problem is that with our masks on, with our personas 'up,' we can't truly show the truth, beauty, and goodness that lie within us. Some of us go through our entire lives living behind our masks. It's a lot of work to always keep our masks on, but we do it to 'save face.'

Conclusion

This gets us back to our original question, how do you know that the *you* that you are showing the world is the real, genuine-article *you* that you truly are, and not just a projected image, just some piece of, or distortion of the true *you*? Healing and spiritual deepening require that you uncover this 'true you' and plunge into God's reservoir of healing power that lays there in wait for you. We'll get to this in chapter three, but first I must tell you a story ... the story of where all this came from.

Chapter Two

The Power of Healing
Your Personality Spiritual Strengths

For 15 years I worked as the Director of Behavioral Sciences at a large teaching hospital. My role was teaching the Family Medicine interns and residents the 'art' of medicine, not the science of medicine. The art of medicine is commonly called 'bedside manner.' This included such topics as: basic counseling skills, diagnostic skills for the many manifestations of depression, anxiety, and other affective disorders, as well as basic family systems intervention skills. Most of all I instructed and modeled so the doctors could adopt a new and broader perspective that allowed them to see a fuller picture of disease. I wanted them to develop a mindset that included factors beyond biology and chemistry as their only reference points in making their overall differential diagnosis. They needed to include emotional, psychological, familial, and relational factors as well as medical data in their treatment planning.

During these 15 years, I came in contact with literally thousands of patients. On selected mornings I would take the medical residents on behavioral science rounds, when we'd visit patients from room to room. The doctors were looking for physical ailments and interested in devising treatment regimens. I was looking for what we referred to then as the psychosocial aspects of the physical disease, factors that may act in conjunction with, or even amplify physical factors and result in symptoms that required care.

When we'd walk into a patient's room, we'd generally find people who were to some degree frustrated or forlorn, depressed or confused, denying, even shameful or guilty. These are some of the common emotional reactions to sickness. Many of these patients seemed to have a nagging, and of course, unrealistic belief that their disease or malady somehow shouldn't be happening. They unconsciously thought of their sickness as an invader or a deception; some saw their sickness as a morbid trick being perpetrated upon them. Some patients even blamed God, which they called by different names. I learned to identify all these various feelings that grew from their internal assessment that what was happening to them was unfair, that somehow this sickness was a fraudulent mistake. Patients would manifest their feelings in many different ways: denial, depression, anxiety, and sometimes anger. At times I'd walk into a room, let's call it room 530, and would feel like the patient was 'spitting venom' because they were so angry at their plight.

At the other end of the spectrum I discovered a small number of patients who seemed to be doing much better than we would otherwise expect. What was so startling to me was that I could walk into the next room, room 531, and feel something entirely different than what I felt in room 530. In this room I found another patient who perhaps had the very same diagnosis, perhaps even receiving the exact same medications, prescribed by the exact same doctors, cared for by the exact same nurses and ancillary personnel as the patient in room 530, but with dramatically different results! I would indeed feel drawn to this person instead of feeling repelled, as I had felt in room 530.

In room 531 I would see someone who was not depressed, denying, forlorn, anxious, angry, or any of the above. Indeed, rather than seeing their sickness as something that needed to be swept away as quickly as possible, as a cruel uninvited intruder into their life that should be banished immediately, the patient in room 531 saw their new diagnosis in an entirely different way, almost as a natural part of the fabric of their life right now. In room 530, the patient wanted only to close this chapter of their life as quickly as possible. But the patient in room 531 seemed to see her/his sickness as the opening of a new chapter of life, a chapter from which she/he could learn more about life. This was far beyond 'normal' patient behavior.

Patients like the one in room 531 weren't happy about being sick, they just seemed to be handling it in a vastly different way. They didn't express delight at being sick, *"Isn't this great, everybody's waiting on me now and this is just what I wanted."* No! They didn't somehow unconsciously desire their heart disease, or their cancer, or their lupus, or their multiple sclerosis, or whatever; they didn't want any of this. Yet in some strange way, in some inexplicable way, they looked at what was happening to them that said, *"This too is a life experience, this too is ultimately something that will make me better."*

I studied these patients with keen interest, and was mystified by what was unfolding right in front of me. I consulted other residents, other doctors and nurses, *"Do you see something different in room 531?"* *"Yes,"* they said, *"we like to go into that room."* So, I knew then that it wasn't only me experiencing the difference. Others were confirming what I saw in room 531, and in other rooms like it. And what was different in room 531, I asked?

As I progressed in my study, I concluded that only about 15% of the patients were like the patient in room 531. The other 85% were communicating, in some way and manner that their sickness shouldn't be happening. But these 15% were identifiably different. I set out to discover, if I could, what caused the difference between the patients that I saw in rooms like 530, and the patients I saw in rooms like 531.

Patients like the one in 531 defied the cultural norms of how patients were 'supposed' to act, they seemed challenged and not angry, zealous and not disgusted, even zestful rather than depressed. They seemed in fact to be using their sickness as some means of achieving greater wholeness, all of which seemed so paradoxical to me. These patients didn't act as though some sort of tragedy had befallen them, they didn't show long morose faces. Nor was there any underlying delight or smugness over the fact that they were suffering from their malady. I wanted to understand them. How could these people remain so full of life, and so centered, while at the same time, their bodies were being ravaged. What was going on?

I considered that these patients might simply be naïve; maybe they just didn't "get it," I wondered. Perhaps they just didn't see that what was going on with them was such a terrible thing.

Perhaps their denial of their sickness was just more hidden than the denial of the others. But these skeptical thoughts didn't answer my question. These patients were truly different.

I came to see these patients as in sync with something well beyond themselves, something that was extraordinary, something that was beyond the physical level ... they seemed transformed. They seemed so comfortable in their own skin. I witnessed their personal depth and their peace, their strength and their inspiration, their inner power, and their confident faces. I came to call such patients; *spiritually healing patients*, because it appeared they had tapped into a power the other 85% didn't seem to have. I continually asked myself, *"What "specialness" had been infused into these patients?"*

Spiritually Healing Patients

I noticed that the other health professionals were drawn to these people too. It seemed to me that these spiritually healing patients were in quiet control of what was going on in their lives. They refused to act as dependent victims of some unknown dark force. There was no self-abasement in them; there was no self-forfeiture, no angst. They didn't exhibit any synthetic form of parochial piety that protected them in some delusional way. There was no pettiness or co-dependent compulsion coming out of these folks. What was it? I wanted to know. And so, I studied, I observed, I looked, I questioned, I talked with them, I listened to them ... and listened some more.

What I eventually came to was most startling, actually it was 'mind-blowing' for me; I wasn't looking for it. But, when all of my qualitative clinical observations were finished, when the data was 'in,' my conclusion became clear, these spiritually healing patients had tapped into power from a very deep place inside them. When I was able to analyze their conceptions, their perceptions, thoughts, feelings, and behaviors together, and viewed it as a whole, what was at the base of their 'secret,' what was the essence of all of their inner stamina, was *spiritual power*. Without even being aware of it, they were using their unique personality spiritual power. They didn't see themselves as special at all; they were just being themselves. Yet their behavior and beliefs were nothing short of profound; what I was seeing in them was the result of a life that had somehow discovered ways of connecting to a transcendent spiritual power source; they were connecting to "the divine" inside them.

These special people had found a new center point of their being, a depth that I could only call Universal Love. I realized that just as these patients were drawn to Love, and came from Love, I too was drawn by Love to the Love within them, and further moved to give love. Giving love and receiving love seems to be the heart's desire of every human, the spiritual life force within us; it seems built right in to our DNA on a spiritual level, just as our material DNA directs the formation of our physical form. Bede Griffiths calls this "the deepest instinct of the soul." (Page 61, Return to the Center).

At the time I was involved in my study, I couldn't say that the medical community held spiritual power in very high clinical regard. I didn't see 'spiritual power' referred to very positively. Even in our larger culture, I didn't pick up news magazines or click to my favorite websites and read much about spiritual power. I've never seen a headline that read: *SPIRITUAL POWER SAVES CITY HALL.* Even today, we give lip service to spiritual energy, but we don't know how it works, we place little trust in it to offer any real power in our lives; we might say we believe, but do we really? It seems that our culture has pretty much relegated spiritual power to a status synonymous with an awkward righteousness, or piety, or head-in-the-clouds religiosity, or even some sort of strident fundamentalism. Yet what I was seeing in patients was honest and direct, quite simple manifestations of spiritual power. As a behavioral scientist trying to be as objective as possible, I found myself questioning my own results. I needed to look deeper, I needed to penetrate beyond the surface of these patients; I needed to touch their 'true' inner reality. These people had it together, each in different ways.

Very gradually, some new vision, some new perception began to overtake me. It seemed as though new eyes opened up within me and I was both surprised and honored to see glimpses of an energy in these patients that I had never seen before. Strangely, I didn't think of this as any kind of special ability, and I still don't. I believe that anyone who is sufficiently motivated, can tap into their unique love-energy, and experience what I experienced. It just became so self-evident to me that spiritual strength was everywhere in these spiritually healing patients. I could talk with one patient and I would 'see' hope; I could talk with another patient and 'see' charity; I could talk with yet another patient and 'see' mercy.

I could talk with other patients and 'see' acceptance, or
steadfastness, or kindness. All of this seemed so natural.
Some of the patients were even terminally sick; they were
dying, and they knew it. But even these terminally sick patients
seemed locked onto some sort of power within them that
defied logical definition; they were trans-form. I found
something inside of me that was drawn to that same
something inside of them, and I knew that whatever was
happening was beyond the material-physical plane.

What is Spiritual Power?

Spiritual power has been defined in many different ways, yet
across cultures we might simply say that spiritual power is
universal love or spirit in action. Love is a cosmic word, a word
that is truly beyond human definition. I've tried to define love a
number of times, and every time I do, it looks so feeble. Love is
so much greater and more dynamic than anything we can
describe on a human level. Love is so big that we can't even see
it directly; all we can see is its behavioral characteristics, its
human manifestations. This of course brings us back to spiritual
power.

I asked myself, were these manifestations that I encountered in
the spiritual healing patients only the surface of their unique
God-given love-energy deep within their soul? When I
encountered the spiritual power of hope in a patient, was I
seeing a part of Universal Love? Is charity a component of Love?
Is mercy also some unit of Love? Is kindness Universal Love in
action? Spiritual power cannot be manufactured on a human
level; it can be practiced on a human level but it doesn't come
from the human level. Spiritual strength comes from a primal

place, an energy source far beyond the human level. If spiritual power finds its source in Universal Love, then does it comes from God? Some might call Universal Love, a higher power (as AA does), or what others might call 'the presence,' or the great 'I am,' or 'the force,' the power of intention,' the law of attraction, or any of many different names that speak to some first source of energy beyond the physical realm. Wherever it originated, this spiritual power takes up residence in each of us, it becomes ours simply because we're human.

Abraham Maslow is one of my favorite psychologists. He's remembered primarily for his ideas about the hierarchy of human needs. Maslow created a psychology based on human potential, the highest level of human functioning. He says that we psychologically grow from our most basic needs, our physical needs, all the way up to our highest needs, what he called self-actualization needs. He ultimately developed his hierarchy of needs from studying the highest levels of human behavior and functioning, which he termed self-actualizing behavior. Maslow's descriptions of people who were self-actualizing, were all functioning on a very transformed, or what psychology calls trans-personal levels. To put it another way, Maslow studied persons functioning on spiritual levels. I followed Maslow's lead in studying the best and the highest functioning persons. I wanted to study the highest spiritually functioning persons, these spiritually healing patients that I encountered on my rounds in the hospital.

Another bright mind that influenced me at the time of my study was Dr. Bernie Siegel, an oncologic surgeon from Yale University. Dr. Siegel had a midlife crisis himself when he was around 45 years old, which forced him to realize that he couldn't continue his work any longer in the ways he had been. He couldn't continue invading peoples' bodies and taking out their cancerous tumors, he couldn't continue irradiating bodies with lethal rays and giving people poison that we call chemotherapy. Dr. Siegel had hit the wall, he'd burnt out. His tragedy led to his own spiritual transformation that eventually catapulted him to become a provocateur of the medical community, trying to spiritualize it. He has gone on to write several best selling books; chief among them is his first book, *Love, Medicine and Miracles*. In this book he talks about a classification of patients that he refers to as *exceptional patients*. Interestingly, he estimates that about 15 percent of the patients that he sees he would call exceptional patients. This of course is the same percentage that I came to call spiritually healing patients in my own study.

Dr. Siegel asserts that exceptional patients are dedicated people who look at disease, not as the kiss of death, but as the opportunity to start living like they never had before. Exceptional patients see their sickness as a wakeup call or a reset button, the opportunity to transform their lives, and participate in their own healing. They remain intensely involved in what's going on; they educate themselves and they demand not to be treated as a disease but rather as a person. In an extraordinary observation, Dr. Siegel points out that exceptional patients dedicate their lives to loving. I noticed much the same phenomenon in my study, spiritually healing patients practiced love-in-action, a force we might call spiritual strength.

Sickness vs. Illness

Before we go on, we must digress a bit to clarify some terms. We need to distinguish between sickness and illness. We use these two words interchangeably as though they referred to the same thing … they don't. Sickness refers to a body part or body system that is broken or malfunctioning in some way. Sickness is the medical diagnosis, that which is 'wrong' with our body.

Illness, on the other hand, is our personal, emotional, psychological, or spiritual reaction to our sickness. Normally one's illness is a negative emotional reaction, which can, if left unattended, cause any number of human maladies from depression, shame, anxiety, anger, submission, denial and any of an array of feelings-based reactions that we think are simply normal consequences of sickness. Of the two, illness is said to cause more pain to the human condition than sickness.

Curing vs. Healing

The next clarification is between curing and healing. The medical community seeks to cure sickness, while the mental health community and to some degree religious institutions seek to heal illness. My research instructed me that spiritual power development did not necessarily cure sickness, but it could go a long way to heal illness.

It was from my research observations that I first formulated the notion that there is expansive potency in this intangible quality called spiritual power, an energy that did not come from the material plane, but rather came from a transpersonal level, a transcendent, spiritual level ... from God. As I completed my work, I identified 30 specific spiritual powers, or what I came to call spiritual strengths, that appeared to be functionally effective in assisting hospital patients reach new levels of healing. Seeing the effect that these spiritual strengths had on the patients that I followed, inspired me to find ways to help the other 85% of patients, who seemed unaware of their spiritual strengths.

Eventually this search led me to construct an assessment-educational questionnaire I called the Healing Gifts Profile (HGP) that could identify a person's unique spiritual strengths. Based on my findings I devised a specialized healing method. For the past 10 years I have taught and certified hundreds of people; nurses, chaplains, counselors, social workers, healing coaches, and others who have used what I now call the *Spiritual Strengths Inner Healing Method*, with literally thousands of persons in physical, mental, or spiritual distress.

Yet it was a much bigger question raised by my inquiries that compelled me to write this book, and modify the HGP into the *Spiritual Strengths Finder*, or SSF, and Spiritual Strengths Healing Method.

If spiritual strengths provide the energy for healing illness, then is it possible that spiritual strengths play a larger role in the human condition, a role that not only positively affects healing, but the entire operation and direction of our personality functioning and our overall well-being in body, mind, and spirit as well?

Chapter Three
Spiritual Strengths as Quantum Healing Energy

If spiritual power provides energy from the center of all energy, and it affects healing in a positive direction, could it also impact the larger personality in similar ways? My research identified spiritual strength as the energy that creates an internal environment, or tipping point that eventually allows a patient to grow toward healing and spiritual deepening. Perhaps spiritual strength is more than the vehicle that delivers the energy to the ill person; perhaps spiritual strength is that energy itself. But where does the energy come from that potentiates our spiritual strengths; what is its source? This question took me in quite a different direction.

A discipline of physics called quantum physics may help us answer this question. Lynne McTaggart has written a beautiful book she simply calls, The Field: The Quest for the Secret Force of the Universe. She does a masterful job in condensing the major findings of quantum physics, and making the esoteric concepts accessible to the lay reader. She says, "*Human beings and all living things are a coalescence of energy in a field of energy connected to every other thing in the world. This pulsating energy field is the central engine of our being and our consciousness, the alpha and the omega of our existence.*"

Quantum physics tells us that life is not simply a chemical reaction, rather life is infused energy; an energy system all arrayed in a vast multitude of forms streaming in and through a cosmic grid, a gigantic energy field. This energy, or life force sustains us; it surrounds us and pervades us, it connects us to everything and everyone. This pervasive, pulsating, sustaining energy field is the love of God.

Quantum physics tells us that everything is energy, and everything else is energy too! What we see with our eyes as matter is actually a vast array of energy pulsating, rotating, evolving, reaching peaks of strength and receding into the larger field of energy. We might call this larger field the energy sphere, the sea of energy from which all energy emerges and to which it returns. Further, all energy is connected to all other energy. Quantum physicists tell us that there are not many energies, instead there is only one pervading energy. All energy seems to flow out from and back to one source in a kind of cosmic respiration. The 'we' that we are then, our bodies, our thoughts, wishes, hopes, sorrows, expectations, friendships, fun, self-esteem, work, and even our spirit is actually all energy, the same energy, yet in different forms.

This new understanding, given to us by quantum physics, expands our view of everything: ourselves, our world, our higher (and lower) cognitive functions, and the cosmos. This new understanding offers us new ways of seeing our existential and operational place in the world. Not only that, this new perspective changes our most basic understanding of how we operate in this vast energy 'soup.'

God is Love … and Love is spiritual energy, or grace.

34

How accurately we connect with this energy sphere, this field, as Lynne McTaggart calls it, determines the quality of our total living experience in body, mind, and spirit. Indeed, the quality of our life meaning rises and falls as our connection with the energy sphere waxes and wanes. Nothing then has any meaning, any existence whatever without connection to this energy field, or energy sphere. There is no such thing as free-floating reality; reality must be linked to, and defined by, the energy field. In order for something to be something, i.e., real, it must be connected to the energy field. When and if something falls away from the field it ceases to be something ... it is nothing, in that it has no existence, no energy.

> Healing power is God's energy.

Energy moves in many ways; the most common type of energy movement that we know of is in waves. The distance between the high point of the energy wave, the peak, and the low point of the wave, or the trough, determines the frequency of the wave. Higher frequency energy waves are said to generate beneficial feelings and thoughts, enabling, or energizing qualities, such as delight, awe, wonder, fondness, attachment, etc. Lower frequency waves generate lower energy that is associated with the more negative thoughts and feelings, such as shame, embarrassment, hatred, guilt, and the like.

At times in our lives we need lower frequency thoughts and feelings. For example, when the car in front of you suddenly stops, you need the lower frequency emotion of fear to motivate you to hit your brakes fast. After this incident you return to your center wave frequency; if you don't, the fear remains in you and eventually you won't want to drive at all.

Likewise, you can increase your wave frequency to damaging levels too. It's personally motivating to become excited about an upcoming event, or an idea, or a relationship, but if you remain in excitement all the time eventually you'll 'burn-out," and lose touch with reality. We always need to return to the middle, where we find our genuine self.

Each of our personality strengths can be conceived of as having a unique wave frequency. At this frequency, or energy level, we are most balanced, most poised, most centered, and most our genuine self. We can move out of this balanced state by going too far away from our central spiritual strength frequency wave in either of two directions. We can, consciously or not, slow down the frequency, or we can speed-up the frequency. In either case we move away from a state of personality balance, or what we call personality coherence, and toward an out-of-balance condition.

Power vs. Force

In a book by this title Dr. David R. Hawkins, M.D. offers a startling proposition based on his years of rigorous and patient-based research. Dr. Hawkins searched for a clearer understanding of the nature of human consciousness, our awareness of our being, our very existence, as well as everything else. His inquiries led him into many fields and sub-fields of science: kinesiology, chaos theory, quantum physics, and nonlinear dynamics, in addition to medicine and psychiatry. What he discovered was not only utterly fantastic, it also relates directly to the central point of this book ... we are spiritually energized uniquely and quite intentionally by God.

Through millions of measurements over the years of his study, Dr. Hawkins discovered that our attitudes and emotions carry power or energy. Further, he calibrated a technique to actually measure varying degrees or levels of power of many different emotions and attitudes. He eventually devised a common quantitative system for comparing various states of consciousness. His system is planned on a number line from 0 to 1000. Any human emotion below 250 such as shame, guilt, grief, fear, desire, anger, pride, etc., drains the human body/system of energy. Emotions above 250 are energy additives or energy attractors, as he calls them. He identified a gradual gradation of emotions above 250, including willingness, acceptance, reason, charity, joy, and peace. Beyond the breakpoint of 700, Dr. Hawkins asserts that we begin to move toward a transcendent enlightenment, a consciousness of things numinous; a 'place' where our world self or the ego self (that self that only knows the world) is gradually gives way to our Holy Self … a sacred bundle of divinity power. It is here in the Holy Self where healing occurs, where God's grace is manifest.

Dr. Wayne Dyer has built upon Dr. Hawkins research and added some of his own philosophical and psychological observations. Dr. Dyer suggests to his readers that, " … *you think of energy in a context of vibration and movement.*" (Page 43, Spiritual Solution …) Like Dr. Hawkins, Dr. Dyer claims that higher spiritual consciousness carries the highest energy vibrations, while what he calls "problem thinking" leads us to low energy vibrations. He goes on, "*The idea here is that a higher frequency will aid in problem solving, whereas a lower frequency will intensify problems and inhibit solutions.*"

Here's an entirely new concept, that healing might simply be shifting the vibration patterns of the six functions of our personality; believing, perceiving, thinking, feeling, deciding, and acting. We can raise the vibration levels of these functions by shifting our focus from those concepts that lower our vibrations to thoughts that raise them. Sounds simple enough, but it takes practice and patience all animated by God's grace.

The process of healing involves an entire conversion of our personality. For example, we gradually learn to shift our beliefs away from the low energy vibrations of despair and/or presumption, to the high-energy vibration of hope; we shift our perceptions away from low vibration complexity and bluntedness, and toward high vibration simplicity; we shift our thoughts away from low vibration notions like inadequacy and/or perfectionism, and toward high vibration thoughts like wisdom ... and so forth. This conversion of our personality functioning involves taking command of our personality in ways that serve to raise the overall energy vibration levels of all six personality functions. We learn to place our mind, our heart, and our soul at the service of our innate spiritual strengths and away from any and all forces that may distract us. We cleanse ourselves of all that pulls us away from the packet of divinity, our spiritual strengths, invested in us.

Personality Coherence

The concept of coherence has been used in different research communities but with surprisingly similar meaning. Dr. Harold Koenig, M.D., a medical researcher at Duke University has studied and written about the impact of spirituality on health for years. He uses the term 'coherence' to denote a condition of internal harmony that emerges when an individual's concept of 'higher power' becomes the lead or director of their lives. The individual has reached a 'place' where they put ultimate and sustaining trust in their higher power, a place where a transcendent sense of order and peace prevails. Most of us experience this coherence only fleetingly, but as we mature spiritually, as we become more receptive to God's grace/power, we can begin to live in coherence almost continuously. When we are 'in coherence' then all our internal energies are aligned and functioning as a whole.

In quantum physics, coherence is used in a different yet analogous way. Quantum coherence refers to a state where subatomic particles (protons, electrons, neutrons, etc.) cooperate together in such a way as to create a new structure. Coherence elevates communication among and between the subatomic particles to such a degree that together they morph into something new. An example of this is one of the mysteries of chemistry; how can two gases, oxygen and hydrogen, come together, or find coherence so sublimely that they now form something fantastically new ... water? Lynn McTaggart likens this communication coherence to all the individual instruments in a symphony orchestra co-acting together in a synergistic way to create something entirely new ... music, in its almost infinite configurations.

Coherence refers to a state of advanced order so rich that the raw material is transformed into something different, something beautiful. The spiritually healing patients that I encountered might be said to have entered some kind of personality coherence, a state where the frequency waves of their spiritual strengths seemed to be vibrating in sync with some higher, perhaps cosmic tuning fork. The specific mode of action that allows all this communication and cooperation among and between energy is of course unknown. Coherence holds your personality together and gives your life the meaning that is your true heart's desire. In the Christian tradition, we could demonstrate the presence of spiritual coherence by adding the Chi Rho, the symbol for Christ, to our model of the personality, like this:

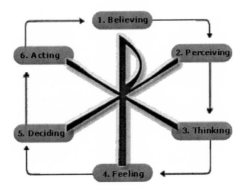

To designate other faith traditions we could insert other symbols at the center of the personality to demonstrate the emergence of coherence, or the development of soul. Jews could use the Star of David, Muslims could use the crescent, and so on.

Water as a Lens

The notion that energy can be communicated on circuits not yet understood is perhaps nowhere more clearly demonstrated than in the research done by Japanese scientist Masaru Emoto. Dr. Emoto first noticed, and then cataloged the differences in frozen water crystals he made and photographed from around the world. He dramatically showed that differences in the ice crystals made from clean, natural water as compared to tainted, polluted, or toxic water. While these differences appeared logical to the scientific mind, the next step of his research did not!

Dr. Emoto expanded his investigations by exposing water to various stimuli: heat, light, music of various types, and finally to words. He found that water exposed to soothing classical music formed ice crystals of stunning beauty, while the same water exposed to rock music formed ice crystals as dissonant as the music. How could this be? What process communicated the music 'energy' to the water? He continued by exposing water to words simply taped to the side of a glass beaker of water. He found that words such as 'harmony,' and 'love,' and 'delight,' and 'peace' formed delicate and beautiful ice crystals. These crystals were marvelously symmetrical, artfully proportioned, and exquisite in their repetitive patterns. The same water exposed to words like 'dread,' and 'shame,' and 'pain,' and 'distrust' created ice crystals that were asymmetrical, disproportional, and with few patterns; crystals that seemed lifeless ... without energy.

Why would water behave so differently when exposed to concepts like the spiritual strengths I had identified in my study, as compared to concepts like the personality shadows and compulsions that represented perversions of the spiritual strengths? Beyond that, by what mechanism and upon what circuits were all these data communicated to the water? What

41

quality of receptivity does water possess that allows it to 'pick-up' data in such an elegant manner? Water, of course, is necessary for life, as we know it here on this material plane. Is the receptivity displayed by water a reflection of the potential receptivity of our own energy system ... our entire organism of body, mind, and spirit?

Universal Love

We formerly defined spiritual strength as universal love in action, indicating that spiritual strength is a benevolent power that flows from the primal source or center of all energy. This source has been called many things by various cultures and philosophies. Chinese culture refers to this universal energy or life force as *qi,* which is akin to the energy sphere or field. Christian tradition might refer to this omnipotent source as *grace*; on another level we simply refer to it universal life spirit. In the *Star Wars* series this energy was called "the force." Anyone who has watched *Star Wars* (who hasn't?) remembers well, *"May the force be with you."* World renowned author and Catholic priest Thomas Keating, who has devoted his ministerial life to the teaching of what he calls centering prayer, lights-up another facet of this energy force for us when he talks about, *"The experience of the Eternal Word as the ultimate source of the universe, as that which is deepest in everything ..."* Noted author and spiritualist Wayne Dyer, says, *"Spirit is what I have chosen to call the formless, invisible energy which is the source and sustenance of life."* (Page 4, There's A Spiritual Solution ...) No matter what it's called, this energy has something to do with what we would call Universal Love. Love is so misunderstood, so misrepresented in our culture; we associate it with eroticism,

42

romanticism, filiality, and sentimentality, but at its heart, love is energy, a force from which all energy radiates. Christianity says this quite simply; God is love.

The so-called Golden Rule perhaps best illustrates the notion that love is the source of all energy. Every religion has its own rendition of the Golden Rule.

Christianity: In everything, do unto others as you would have them do to you. New Testament, Matthew 7:12.

Taoism: Regard your neighbor's gain as your own gain, and your neighbor's loss as your own loss. Lao Tzu, *T'ai Shang Kan Ying P'ien*, 213-218.

Confucianism: One word which sums up the basis of all good conduct ... loving-kindness. Do not do to others what you do not want done to you. Confucius, *Analects* 15.23.

Buddhism: Treat not others in ways that you yourself would find hurtful. The Buddha, *Udana-Varga* 5.18.

Hinduism: This is the sum of duty: do not do to others what would cause pain if done to you. *Mahabharata* 5:1517.

Islam: Not one of you truly believes until you wish for others what you wish for yourself. The Prophet Muhammad's *Hadith*.

Judaism: What is hateful to you, do not do to your neighbor. This is the whole <u>Torah</u>; all the rest is complementary. Hillel, *Talmud, Shabbat* 31a

Sikhism: I am a stranger to no one, and no one is a stranger to me. Indeed, I am a friend to all. Guru Granth Sahib, p. 1299.

All these religious traditions, and cultural directives seem to flow from a singular source; there appears an overarching, even universal quality about them even though the contexts from which they sprang were/are all quite different. Somehow by treating one's fellow humans with respect creates peace and opens us to a harmony that offers rewards both interactively with others, and intra-actively within ourselves. Peace and harmony, of course, are spiritual strengths, indeed, two of the 30 spiritual strengths I identified as 'healing spiritual strengths' in my study at the hospital.

Perhaps when we actively and intentionally shift ourselves toward universal energy (call it love) we attract benefits to ourselves and to others that otherwise would lie fallow. When we lean toward this love-energy, we create a new balance within ourselves that harmonizes, aligns, stabilizes, centers, and synchronizes our internal energy field that quite naturally, simultaneously, and effortlessly improves our health in body, mind, and spirit. Might this be the operative action of personality coherence?

The Diamond

In my thoughts and meditations on the meaning of love and its derivatives that I call spiritual strengths, I use an image of a diamond to help me center myself. A diamond is the most brilliant gemstone in the world. When we position a diamond toward the sun, light energy flows into the stone of the diamond. This light energy is refracted within the stone, and is then reflected off the many facets of the stone. Other gemstones perform the same function, but a diamond does it best.

In my imagination, the stone of the diamond is your personality, and each facet of the stone is a unique spiritual strength. I liken the light energy coming from the sun to universal energy emanating from the first source of all energy. The various spiritual strengths are the facets of the stone. Each and every one of your spiritual strengths is distinct; one may overlap with other strengths, yet it retains its individual uniqueness. At the same time, each facet is a part of the stone of the diamond; each facet is separate and distinct. The diamond could not sparkle without the facets, and, of course, the facets could not reflect apart from the stone; one could not work without the other. Yet, a diamond, even a well cut and polished diamond, cannot sparkle on its own; it needs light. A diamond could not sparkle, could not realize its potential, if it were kept in a drawer. Likewise, if our very essence and our source of Universal Love is not expressed, then we cannot sparkle in our uniquely personal way, as we are intended, without positioning ourselves toward this love-energy. When we intentionally contemplate, or otherwise think about a spiritual ideal, a spiritual power, or virtue, we set in spiritual motion the actual manifestation of this power in our life. This is the job of your unique spiritual strengths.

Chapter Four

The Forces of Your Personality:
Strengths, Shadows, and Compulsions

Personality Spiritual Strengths

Your spiritual strengths are the central activating powers of
your personality. Your spiritual strengths reside within you; they
are part of you, indeed, your spiritual strengths form the
essence of you. Your spiritual strengths originate from the
essential power of the universe, what could be called love, or
grace, or *qi*, etc. This fact makes you a reflector of the energy of
Universal Love. You represent cosmic power; you are a carrier
of life and light, exquisitely unique; a special agent, an emissary
of the source of all energy – God!

Your spiritual strengths were given to you as pure gift; you had
no part whatever in their bestowal. Your only responsibility in
life, and the central healing action, is to express your gifts, your
spiritual strengths, in your little corner of the world. As you
successively unfold your spiritual strengths, both to yourself and
to others, you become stronger, more potent, capable, and
more involved in life. In this sense, your sojourn here on earth
can be seen as a hero's journey. You confront the challenges,

tackle the adventures, engage the dragons and demons that befall you, and the trials that your life reveals. Healing and optimal living means that with God's grace you gradually overcome life's challenges by uncovering more and more of the authentic you, and by accurately and purposefully focusing the love-energy you find there. Eventually you arrive at a point and place of personal integrity, a spiritual wholeness that represents the fullest realization of your spiritual strengths.

Your spiritual strengths offer you special guidance; they nudge you toward healing your essential fragmentation, and guide you toward greater personal and spiritual fulfillment. You can ignore your spiritual strengths or you can ignite them, you can capture them or censor them, exploit them or expedite them; the choice is always yours.

Together your six spiritual strengths constitute your special formula or prescription for success, individuality, and authenticity. Your six spiritual strengths are a potent soul power enabling you to subdue all other opposing forces that may befall you. Your six spiritual strengths form a unit of love-energy that is the uniqueness of you! Your strengths are the central stabilizers and stimulators of the spiritual stamina or grit in you; they are the deep keels that keep your personality heading in the direction of healing.

Personality Strengths and You

In chapter one we discussed how your personality operates by the action of six different functions: 1) believing, 2) perceiving, 3) thinking, 4) feeling, 5) deciding, and 6) acting. The operation of these six functions is sequential. For example, a feeling doesn't arrive from nowhere and from nothing; a feeling has reality because it is the result of a particular belief in your belief core becoming activated. This (1) belief in-turn gives definition, or frames your view of whatever you perceive. Your unique (2) perception then generates a thought. The (3) thought moves you to experience a feeling (or feelings) that is the natural consequence of that thought. The (4) feelings have but one job, to motivate (5) decisions. And, of course, we could have no (6) actions or behaviors without decisions.

No part of the personality functions in isolation; the six functions operate best when they find coherence with one another. Personality coherence emerges when your unique spiritual strengths operate in concert. Coherence requires energy. My research indicates that this energy comes from the personality-specific spiritual strengths that power your personality functions.

When you took the *Spiritual Strengths Finder* (I hope you did) you discovered that you had a unique spiritual strength for each of your six personality functions; this strength is your premier spiritual power for that particular personality function. These six premier strengths constitute your spiritual fingerprint, the unique qualities invested in you by God. These are the qualities that continuously seek expression in your world.

1) Believing: Your premier believing strength provides the psychic or soul energy required to 'run' your believing function. Your beliefs, assumptions, attitudes, values, etc. are energized by this strength. Your believing strength is the most potent

force in you that fortifies and gives power to your own beliefs. This strength gives you courage of conviction, the confidence required to make internal commitments and develop a philosophy of living. Your premier believing spiritual strength stands as the pivotal power at the core of your mind.

2) Perceiving: Your premier perceiving strength gives you the power to 'see' yourself, others, the world, etc. most accurately. This strength enables you to 'frame' all the stimuli 'out there' in ways that will be most beneficial for you ultimately. This strength is like a lens through which your vision is corrected giving you 'right sight.' It allows you to see the beautiful person that you are; certainly it also lets you see what needs changing. Focusing on what needs changing is also part of your beauty. True perception emerges when you center your vision on the soothing power of your perceiving strength. Your premier perceiving strength beckons you to look beyond the transience of the world and onto more changeless reality.

3) Thinking: Your premier spiritual strength of your thinking function permeates your higher cognitive process including analysis, evaluation, and assessment. This strength gives you the power to make the best possible sense out of the perceptions you derive from your environment; it injects meaning into the events of your life. Your thinking strength actually determines the kind of world in which you live, because your world is much more 'in your head' than it is 'out there.' Your thinking strength allows you to think in a whole manner, considering all the forces and factors that need to be fully and thoroughly considered. This premier thinking strength lets you 'judge' yourself and others most clearly, fairly, and completely.

4) Feeling: Your premier feeling function spiritual strength energizes your emotions; it gives you the energy to become fully aware of your feelings, and the power to shape your feelings in service of your onward development. Your strength allows you to transform paralyzing feelings into more enabling ones that can emotionally position you closer to your authentic personality. Your feelings strength gives you more sensitivity to the potential impact of your emotions, both positively and negatively. It offers you ways of freeing yourself from paralyzing feelings rather than 'stuffing' them.

5) Deciding: Your premier spiritual strength in your deciding function moves you to 'right choice;' it frees your will from whatever confinement may be hindering it. Your deciding strength gives you the opportunity to become more aware of the necessary choices in your life and gives you the power to make them. Your strength saves you from indecision, it propels proper choice; it turns you away from the potential chaos of indecision and lets you embrace a solid free will. Your strength offers strategies, identifies goals and objectives, formulates a life purpose, and develops priorities that move you in the direction of personality coherence.

6) Acting: Your premier acting spiritual strength allows you to be sure of your behaviors, more constant, confident and purposeful. Your strength leads you toward actions for your ultimate personality alignment. Your strength gives you more command over your conduct rather than forfeiting it to others; it lets you take responsibility for your actions because you are more aware of what needs doing. Your strength allows you to tackle what need doing in a 'first things first' manner. Your

premier acting spiritual strength is that creative spark inside you that motivates you to actualize your potentials.

Paradoxical Personality Balance

The personality seeks harmony within itself; it strives to make evenness or balance a reality, but it seems to do it in ways that are dramatically paradoxical. The so-called law of personality balance holds that when a trait is consciously developed or taught, and the personality accepts it as a part of itself, quite automatically and unconsciously, the <u>opposite</u> of the trait is imprinted onto the inner world of the personality. In his landmark book, <u>Make Friends with Your Shadow</u>, author William Miller, illustrates this law when he says, *"For example, if a child finds in his environment that it is to his advantage to develop the qualities of submissiveness, obedience, quietness, and docility, then the opposite qualities of rebelliousness, stubbornness, and independence will be tucked away at the inner world end of the psyche and perhaps one day will quite unexpectedly come breaking through to the outer world and surprise everyone, the person himself included."* (Page 16) The more strongly a quality becomes a functional part of our personality, the more strongly its opposite will also find ways of worming itself into your personality.

You gravitate to those personality traits that receive positive reinforcement, attention, confirmation, or even affection from your environment; when others praise a particular trait or action; you quite naturally, and without any conscious thought, go to work incorporating that trait into your personality. This works pretty well for you in that it enables you to conform to many different situations. Yet, just as the science of physics teaches that every action has an equal and opposite reaction, this same kind of process is at work within your personality.

All positive personality strengths seem to be balanced by an opposing negative force or forces. The development of any spiritual strength in your personality seems to beget the reactive emergence of its opposite as a kind of psychological sidecar. These sum total of all these emergent reactive forces make-up what Dr. Karl Jung, and his Jungian followers, refer to as the shadow of the personality. Jung concluded that you conveniently submerge all unwanted thoughts, impulses, urges, etc. that you are barred from incorporating into your public persona or personality mask, by social convention or moral directives, underneath the 'waterline' of your psyche. All this reactive 'fear' material may be out of sight, but it is certainly not out of mind. These submerged shadows live on under the placid surface of your persona-protected daily life only to break through in times of personal tension or stress. My research instructs me that you have not just one overarching shadow that contains all the negative reactive material, as Dr. Jung has postulated, instead you have six specific shadows, one for each of your six spiritual strengths of your personality.

Personality Shadows: looking into the face of your dark side

Each of your six spiritual strengths also has a corresponding characteristic, or behavioral weakness called a shadow. A shadow is the reverse image of your strength; what your strength is, your shadow is not, and vice versa. A shadow is a 'place' in your personality where your spiritual strength is absent, a 'space' in you where your strength is not. Your spiritual strengths are pure energy, but your shadows are devoid of energy, instead they constitute what I call dysenergy. While your spiritual strengths are all spiritual energy, Universal Love in action, your shadows are all vices, or fear in reaction. Your shadows act like personality vulnerabilities in you; they cause you to stumble over the same problems that have chronically tripped you up, they move you away from your strengths and toward you weaknesses. Your shadows can sabotage you, or more accurately they cause you to sabotage yourself.

Your shadows pull you toward the most impotent places within you; they push you to your points of personal insufficiency. When you move away from your strengths you create a vacuum inside you that is filled by one of your six shadows. This creates a condition where you are 'living in your shadows.' Shadows are personality blind spots in that you are only rarely aware that you have moved toward, or into a shadow. Shadows act like terrorists; you don't know they are at work until the damage is done. Shadows attempt to pull energy from your spiritual strengths. If left unattended, your shadows could eventually overpower your spiritual strengths and take over your personality. Shadows are the 'underside' or "backside" of your spiritual strengths. The paradox of shadows is that the more potent your strengths, the more troublesome will be your shadows, as you shall see more clearly in future chapters.

You are fearful and ashamed of your shadows because they are the opposite of what you're trying to project into the world, consequently, you do everything you can to hide your shadows.

Your shadows contain everything you don't want others to know about you. Interestingly you are generally blind to your shadows as well, you repress them, try to push them away, even convince yourself that they don't really exist. Yet, that nagging fear that there's more of you than what you show to the world, and that this 'more' is not something very nice, haunts you. You try to get rid of this fear usually by projecting it onto other people, or things, or institutions. Religion and the government are common recipients of your shadow projections. You blame everyone and everything else for your fears that you know in your heart are really yours to claim.

Yet the shadow can manifest itself in many noxious ways, it can resist the personality spiritual strength directly, in which case we call it the shadow of the strength. On the other hand, this negative force might show itself by carrying the strength too far, pushing the strength overboard as it were, and therefore perverting the strength into something quite frightening. We call this perversion of the spiritual strength, a compulsion.

Personality Compulsions: the other side of your dark side

Each of your six spiritual strengths is accompanied not only by a shadow, but also by a *compulsion*. As your shadows are the absence of your spiritual strengths, your compulsions are the perversion of your strengths. Compulsions result when you attempt to use your strengths in inappropriate ways, when you exaggerate your spiritual strengths and contort them into forces that actually work against you. For example, hope is a marvelous spiritual strength, but it can be contorted into a damaging force when you exaggerate and distort it into the personality compulsion of presumption, taking someone or something for granted. Presumption disrupts your inner peace; it separates you from others and from your universal source of energy.

Your compulsions are the opposite of your shadows, and yet just as damaging to your ultimate growth and development. A compulsion results when you misuse your spiritual strengths by bringing them to their most illogical extension. You move toward your compulsions when you stridently and egotistically over-attempt to use your spiritual strengths for your own benefit only, and in so doing not only forget about the needs of others, but dismiss their needs altogether. The subconscious quality of your compulsions means you are most often blind to them. This fact makes compulsions all the more insidious, difficult to detect, and hard to wrestle. Compulsions distort your strengths, they separate you from the growth power of your strengths; they break your communion with your authentic self and with the power of universal love.

Shadows and compulsions are powerful forces, yet they do not dictate your personality because they are only proclivities or inclinations, not directives. While the shadows and compulsions are resident in your personality, they may never, or only infrequently, be expressed. They may lie dormant for years or even a full lifetime. They are more prone to activate when you're stressed, when you begin reacting to life instead of responding. When you're stressed you're more at risk of slipping out of your personality center strengths position, and into your shadows or compulsions. Assuming a mental posture of mindful wakefulness about the working of your personality can give you clues or cues as to how your shadows and compulsions might be manifesting in your life and how to turn back to your spiritually motivating center position.

Here is an example of the spiritual strengths, shadows, and compulsions in each of the six personality functions of an actual person. I offer this only as a point of comparison and reference, not as an ideal personality, of the power of personality centering.

Personality Function	Personality Compulsions	Spiritual Strengths	Personality Shadows
Believing	presumption	HOPE	despair
Perceiving	bluntedness	SIMPLICITY	complexity
Thinking	perfectionism	WISDOM	inadequacy
Feeling	ingratiating	EMPATHY	obtuseness
Deciding	unreality	TRANSCENDENCE	worldliness
Acting	arrogance	COURAGE	timidity

<<< >>>

In Medio Stat Virtus… In the Middle Stands the Power

Notice that the spiritual strengths are in the center position of the personality, and the shadows and compulsions are at the extremes. Tensions and stress, especially from sickness or brokenness or any kind, can push you away from your spiritual strengths; they can push and pull you toward your shadows or compulsions. Yet, it's when you're 'in the middle' of your personality, in your strengths, you are at your very best. Your

57

spiritual strengths possess your personal power, the power you need to operate your personality optimally and be open to their healing balm. Your shadows and compulsions have no power in themselves, but they do have dysenergy, or anti-power to pull and push you off your center position. The theological principle, first stated by St. Thomas Aquinas in Latin, *In medio stat virtus,* in the middle stands the power, the energy, the virtue, or the spiritual strength, serves as the conceptual underpinning for a more dynamic understanding of the mechanics of the personality.

You can't be at your center, at your best, all the time. Yet, as you mature, as you develop ever-deeper sensitivity and grow toward personality coherence, you naturally spend less time out in the shadows and compulsions and more time in the solid middle of your personality. Personality coherence emerges in you when you manage to bring all your strengths together into an elegant harmony. Such synchronization of your spiritual strengths is only rarely possible, yet when it happens you enter into a 'zone' or 'flow' of maximum personality power.

Life Lessons

Life confronts us with so many forces that tend to push us off the center position of our solid core, our spiritual strengths. This is why it's so important for you to embrace your spiritual strengths, to become evermore aware of them as they operate in your everyday life, and to celebrate them with continuous gratitude. In ways such as these you will find your best, most accurate healing personality; you will gradually align yourself with what Dr. Wayne Dyer calls the universal power of intention. You'll become increasingly aware of how your personality shadows and compulsions have held you captive, how they have kept your authentic personality strengths from bringing out the best in you.

As this process of personal enlightenment and healing unfolds, your genuine self will take the lead of your personality more and more, until there comes a time when the real you will finally take the reins of your personality. The spiritually healing patients in my study had already grown through this process when I encountered them in their hospital rooms. They were 'in charge' of their personalities, their beliefs, perceptions, thinking, feelings, decisions, and their behavior. The more you focus your personal compass toward the center of your personality, toward your spiritual strengths, the more you will manifest your authentic self and find healing therein.

One of the ways you can learn who you are, and come to know your genuine strengths even better is to recognize your shadows and compulsions that stand as dark sentinels on either side of your strengths. Shadows and compulsions must not be viewed with fear or angry disdain causing you to run from them or to work obsessively to sweep them out of your personality. Rather, you do well to give credence to your shadows and compulsions as the potential forces they are in your life, albeit dysenergy forces. Make no mistake about the fact that your shadows and compulsions are spiritual forces in themselves; more accurately, they are spiritual anti-forces. They can cause real damage to you; this fact will become more evident as you progress in this book.

Shadows and compulsions are permanent parts of your personality; they cannot be swept from your life, they are here to stay. Indeed, the more you try to obliterate them the stronger they 'come on.' When you try to turn away from your shadows and compulsions, when you deny their existence, you're rendering yourself blind, and paradoxically more vulnerable to their action in your life. You can inadvertently give them more force and, consequently, diminish the power of your spiritual strengths. The old adage, "Those who live by the sword, die by the sword," may describe a facet of this paradoxical situation. When you invest so much energy into anything, it begins to consume you and undermines the very strengths that make you unique, whole and integrated; you begin to lose your very self.

It's best if you can get to know your shadows and compulsions very well, become aware of how they manifest themselves in your life, how they act and interact. You need to be 'in touch' with your shadows and compulsions, otherwise you risk becoming overly influenced and pressured by them without your consciously knowing it. You need to give your shadows and compulsions their due, if not you suffer their consequences; when you try to deny them they begin to have internal 'temper tantrums.' Failing to acknowledge them, only gives them more potency. If you try to muzzle your shadows and compulsions through denial or projection, repression or displacement, you will sooner or later feel these dark sides of your personality making ever-louder 'noises' to come out. Ever keener awareness of your shadows and compulsions allows you to make choices that are healthier, more complete, more practical, and ultimately more effective. You are incomplete without your shadows and compulsions, in a strange twist of logic; you need them to heal.

Shadows and compulsions always point to the power of your spiritual strengths. You wouldn't have the shadows and compulsions that you do if you didn't possess your unique spiritual strengths. The more adept you become in recognizing how your shadows and compulsions work in your personality the better you can use this information as clues or cues to gently turn yourself around back to your spiritual strengths. Your shadows and compulsions then can serve as guides in reverse, instead of pointing the way to go, they serve you by pointing the opposite way to go. This is important information you can learn to interpret well as you pick your way through the mystery of your life.

Shadows and compulsions help define who you are; they provide you with the grist for growth. Miller says it well, *"Accept it (them: shadows and compulsions) and take its (their) existence into account, learn its (their) qualities and intentions, realize that in its (their) ambiguity and paradox it (they) is (are) to be 'suffered' and used constructively."* (Page 115, Make Friends with Your Shadow)) It is in the tension that emerges between your shadows and your spiritual strengths, as well as between your compulsions and your strengths, where you will find the motive power for healing and spiritual development. Your job is not to avoid your shadows and compulsions; rather your job is to use your shadows and your compulsions as wake-up calls for you to begin redirecting your life in ways you probably never thought about before. Yet, Karl Jung warned us that while recognition of the shadows (and compulsions) is necessary for advanced self-awareness, the very process of becoming more conscious of them will challenge the ego-based personality. As you continue your growth process of heightened awareness of your shadows and compulsions you may cause further tension in your personality as your ego "circles its wagons" to protect its control over your personality.

Part Two

Your Personality Comes to Life

While *Part One* of this book gave you a somewhat theoretical overview of your personality, in *Part Two* we move to a personal level where we examine all the parts of your personality with a much finer adjustment on your personality microscope. The 12 chapters in *Part Two* are divided into six, two-chapter sections, with each of these six sections devoted to one of the six functions of the personality. The first chapter in each section thoroughly describes that particular personality function, while the second chapter gives definitions of each of the spiritual strengths in that function together with short stories that give "flesh" to the strengths, shadows, and compulsions.

Chapter Five

Personality Function One

Believing: *Your Internal Operating System*

Brokenness and wounding do not occur in order to break human dignity, but to open the heart so God can act.
Martin Marty

The first step toward healing is correcting any inaccurate beliefs that may be blocking your spiritual progression. A belief is an idea that you have adopted as a certainty. The number and variety of beliefs you hold is almost endless. When you raise a concept to a belief you no longer question its veracity ... it is simply a belief. Of course there are various degrees of certainty that we give to our many beliefs. On the simplest level are common beliefs; these include how to get along in our environment in practical ways. Examples of common beliefs would be, the best way to get to the airport, the best way to get along with any angry person, the best way to teach children, and so forth. These are all common beliefs, not because everybody believes as you do, but because you've incorporated these ideas into your belief core as effective means for getting a task accomplished.

The next level of belief is the ideas you hold onto with commitment, ideas about which you are zealous. Examples might be your political party, ideas about your occupation or profession, concepts about property ownership, your favorite sports team, right and wrong, acceptable behavior in yourself and others, and so forth. Beyond this level of belief is the highest level of certainly that might be termed what you simply "know" to be true. A newspaper reporter asked well-known psychotherapist Dr. Carl Jung whether he believed in God. He hesitated for some time before he answered, *"No, I don't believe in God,"* he responded, *"I <u>know</u> there is God!"*

Dr. Theodore Millon is probably the reigning 'guru' of personality theory in the psychological community today. Dr. Millon has done more research, writing, and teaching about the basic underpinnings, the intricacies, the variabilities, and the constancies of personality than anyone else. His special understanding of, and sensitivity to personality allows him to write eloquently about his chosen focus. Here is how Dr. Millon describes the believing function of the personality. Beliefs are:

- Unconscious premises of the mind

- Distinctly personal expectations and assumptions

- Unarticulated rules and dispositional inferences

- Internal schemata, operating system, framework, scaffolding

- Dispositional sets

- Unconscious matrix or inner templates

Dr. Andrew Newberg, director of the Center for Spirituality and the Mind at the University of Pennsylvania is very clear about the believing function when he says, *"The brain is a believing machine because it has to be. Beliefs affect every part of our lives. They make us who we are. They are the essence of our being."*

Your Beliefs form the foundation of your personality; beliefs strongly influence how you use the other five functions of your personality. Beliefs determine what you value; indeed your values and your attitudes are higher order components of your belief core. Beliefs are:

- The basis of your personality

- The definition of who your are

- Your fundamental assumptions

- The building blocks of your value system

- Your guiding life principles

- All your basic definitions of life and living

- The basic tenets of your faith

- Your secure convictions

Where do beliefs come from?

Your beliefs come from a number of sources. Dr. Jung maintained that you are born with certain pre-conceptions of life experience that you received through your ancestry over the millennia of human history. He calls this concept your 'collective unconscious.' His theory maintains for example that you're born with the concept of 'mother' already imprinted on your belief core. Because so many humans have had mothers, you enter the world with this pre-notion securely intact.

You also learn, or develop your beliefs. Most of us have parents, and have attended school for the greater part of our formative years. These early life experiences poured many, many beliefs into your belief core. You also develop beliefs from experience. How many times do you need to touch a hot stove to come to the belief that such action is not good for you? How many times do you need to be shamed or embarrassed before you formulate the belief that you'll want to avoid such situations in the future? You develop beliefs from the media. How is your belief core molded by the hours of television you watch, or the time you spend surfing on the internet, or listening to talk shows, or simply reading highway billboards?

You hold on to some of your beliefs for your entire life, but many, if not most, you change as your life progresses. If you didn't change some of your beliefs you couldn't grow, you couldn't mature. When you were a baby you believed (albeit unconsciously) that you were utterly dependent on your parents. This belief was quite necessary at that time, but if you didn't change this belief, how would you ever achieve independence and mature?

Have you ever wondered why you remember some events in your life so clearly, but you can't remember what happened five minutes before or after this impressed memory? You remember best at these times when you added, subtracted, or otherwise changed a belief or set of beliefs. It's as though you took an internal snapshot of the event, and filed it away with an extra-added emotional charge attached to it, a charge that allows you to retrieve the event as a memory much easier than other events in your life. Something shifted in your belief core at that point in time, you came to a new realization, a new understanding about yourself, about others, or about the world; this new conceptualization required you to rearrange your belief core. When you change or add a belief, you place a special accent on the event that served as the setting for the change; certainly this is memorable. You may not remember what beliefs you changed but you do remember the event because of its startling emotional valence.

Any success requires that you change your beliefs. For example, you may have, at one time or another, been on a diet to lose some weight, so many of us have. Were you successful in the short run and less successful over the long haul? Every diet 'works,' at least to some degree, some diets may be more effective for you than others, but most diets do work. Then why is it so easy to put the lost weight right back on? The answer is simple. While you changed your eating behavior for the short-run when you were dieting, you neglected to dig deeper into yourself, your belief core, where you could change your beliefs about food and your beliefs about the behavior of eating. Once you formulate a more accurate (healthy) belief structure about what food means, and modify the purpose of why you eat, you will keep the weight off. Changing beliefs is the basis for any personal success.

Well-known author, television personality, and thought provocateur Anthony Robbins offers six beliefs that he says are his principles for personal success. I offer them here not as an endorsement but simply to illustrate the power of belief.

1. Everything happens for a reason and a purpose, and everything that happens serves us.

2. There is no such thing as a failure. There are only results.

3. Whatever happens ... take responsibility.

4. It's not necessary to understand everything in order to use everything.

5. People are your greatest resource.

6. Work is play.

Robbins claims that these are transformational beliefs that will make you successful to the degree that you can incorporate them into your belief core. Naturally you'll need to simultaneously throw-out any opposing beliefs, otherwise you'll suffer from intra-psychic dissonance, when one set of beliefs contradicts others. We'll cover more on this later.

Change in the believing function requires energy

In order to change your beliefs and attitudes about anything you need personal power in the form of energy, life energy. Where does this energy come from? This brings us to a fundamental question of this book, what powers your personality? Certainly your personality is not run on the same fuel that powers your organic structure, or bodily systems and organs. It's not your breakfast cereal that powers, or energizes your personality; it's energy from an entirely different source.

Change of any sort requires stamina, determination, and the power of the universe, the universal power of Love, or what we call spiritual strength on the personality level. For example, to change your attitudes about food and about the behavior of eating you need to tap into an energy source far beyond what willpower alone can offer; you need to tap into that universal power source and translate this energy into your spiritual strengths. In order to change your beliefs, this energy needs to flow into the believing function of your personality. So, where do you get it?

My research in the hospital taught me that spiritual strength is energy, flowing from the first source and center of all energy -- God. Upon further investigation it became clear that each of the six functions of the personality had its own unique, essential energy, a salient personal power, or what I now call the *premier spiritual strength* of that particular personality function. This means that each of us has six premier spiritual strengths, one for each of the six functions of the personality. Look at the figure below, notice that there are five spiritual strengths subsumed under each of the six functions of the personality, for a total of 30 spiritual strengths.

Personality Spiritual Strengths

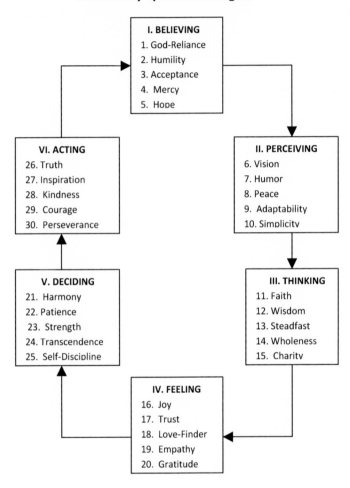

I. BELIEVING
1. God-Reliance
2. Humility
3. Acceptance
4. Mercy
5. Hope

VI. ACTING
26. Truth
27. Inspiration
28. Kindness
29. Courage
30. Perseverance

II. PERCEIVING
6. Vision
7. Humor
8. Peace
9. Adaptability
10. Simplicity

V. DECIDING
21. Harmony
22. Patience
23. Strength
24. Transcendence
25. Self-Discipline

III. THINKING
11. Faith
12. Wisdom
13. Steadfast
14. Wholeness
15. Charity

IV. FEELING
16. Joy
17. Trust
18. Love-Finder
19. Empathy
20. Gratitude

I was amazed at how easily the 30 spiritual strengths almost classified themselves among the six personality functions. Without strain or disharmony, and with very little effort, the 30 strengths arranged themselves evenly among the personality functions. As easily as dairy cows find their correct stalls each

72

evening as they enter the barn for milking, the 30 strengths fell into their correct personality slots automatically. Certainly some spiritual strengths could find a home in more than one personality function. The spiritual strength of faith, for example could 'fit' just as easily in the believing function as in the thinking function, but the internal concept of loyalty, so central to faith, slotted this spiritual strength most snugly in the thinking function. Other spiritual strengths could easily do 'double duty' like faith could, but a closer look made the decision to move them seamlessly into the function where they rested best. The very smoothness of this classification process was in itself a confirmation of the validity of the selection process.

Spiritual Strengths as Ideals

You'll notice that the descriptions of spiritual strengths, shadows and compulsions in the next chapter are behavioral in nature. These virtuous behaviors are the secondary effect of the energy of the spiritual strength; the behaviors themselves are not the spiritual strength itself. For example, the fruits or behaviors that are considered merciful only flow from the energy of the spiritual strength implicit in the spiritual strength of mercy. Mercy, as any of the spiritual strengths, is spiritual energy itself. Acting merciful is certainly a cultural 'good,' or what we could call a civic spiritual strength, a socially positive way of acting. This is contrasted with the spiritual strength of mercy that is a energy that flows from universal power (universal love). This spiritual energy in the spiritual strength is the motive power of your personality; the more you are in the energy of your spiritual strengths, the more you are in your true Self, the more you are 'in love.'

We seek love, indeed we crave love; our heart's desire is to be 'in love.' The concept here of 'being in love' is quite a different concept than the notion of 'falling in love,' which conjures up images of romantic connections, or some spontaneous quake of the emotions where one is swept into an ecstasy of positive feelings and can act in ways that may even seem irrational; such is the human condition. Yet this romantic love, as wonderful and desirous at it appears, is only a facsimile of universal love … the power that calls us to go home.

Spiritual strengths are ideals; you can never fully assimilate them into your personality. By definition, spiritual strengths can never be fully practiced or achieved perfectly here on this earthly plane. Anyone who has tried to practice perfect patience eventually grows impatient with trying to practice patience perfectly, and is sooner or later coerced to acknowledge the utter futility of the undertaking. No, spiritual strengths are ideals; just because you have been infused with them doesn't mean that you, by sheer force of your will, can bring them to their highest manifestation. But, just because we can't practice spiritual strengths perfectly doesn't mean we should just give-up on them as impossible; there is much, much to gain by folding them into your life as best we can each day.

Discovering healing begins when you pursue truth. When the truth of your spiritual strengths is brought to your shadows and compulsions, the truth, the power of Universal Love, always prevails. Healing requires that you refrain from attacking your shadows and compulsions directly as foreign invaders of your personality, rather you bring the truth of your spiritual strengths to your shadows and compulsions; when you do they will fade into the background because they will be overcome by the light of truth.

Now let's take a look at the actual strengths, shadows, and personality compulsions of the believing function, together with some stories that give you an insight into how these can work in your life.

Chapter Six

The Five Spiritual Strengths, Destructive Shadows, and Damaging Compulsions of the Believing Function of the Personality

Here are the five spiritual strengths of the believing function of the personality, along with their corresponding shadows and compulsions. One of these strengths is your premier strength, the guiding strength of your believing function. You identified your premier believing strength when you took the *Spiritual Strengths Finder*. Of course, you're also most vulnerable to the shadow and compulsion that stand as foreboding anti-energies on either side of your premier strength.

Believing Function
Compulsion ....Spiritual Strength ....Shadow

dependency <<<<<<< God Reliance >>>>>>   doubt

self-abasement <<<<< Humility >>>>>>>>> self-centeredness

aloofness <<<<<<<<< Acceptance >>>>>>>> dissension

legalism <<<<<<<<<< Mercy >>>>>>>>>>>> indifference

presumption <<<<<<< Hope >>>>>>>>>>>> despair

1) God Reliance is ...

- Placing the full store of your belief in the ultimate benevolence of God
- Centering your value system on God
- Finding your security in union with God
- Finding strengthened certainty and conviction in God's hand
- Discovering your personal confidence in, and investing your ultimate assurance in God

The shadow of God Reliance is doubt ...

1. Disputable, questionable, suspect
2. Being dubious, feeling uncertain, and becoming incredulous
3. Distrustful, suspicious, heretical
4. Unbelief, incredulous, skeptical
5. Faithless, uncertain
6. Incredible, inconceivable, fallible
7. Desire to control the uncontrollable
8. Premature disengagement
9. Rush to judgment
10. Self-imposed isolation

The compulsion of God Reliance is dependency ...

1. Needing excessive positive regard from others (working the crowd)
2. Seeing one's value only in terms of those around you
3. Scaling back one's sense of personal independence

4. Subordination of your spirit to the desires of others
5. Relying on the beliefs and convictions of others rather than independently placing your conviction in God
6. Risk avoidance
7. Compelled to indecision
8. Giving over all decisions to others
9. Emotional numbness
10. Emotional paralysis

Low Self Esteem
Laura's Story

dependency <<<<<<< God Reliance >>>>>>>>> doubt

Laura hung-up the phone and she immediately broke into tears. Her sister Sonja had just done it again, berated Laura for imaginary transgressions and omissions that Laura 'could have' foreseen or 'should have' prevented. Sonja was a master at cornering Laura into thinking that she was a 'bad' sister, uncaring, indifferent, and self-centered; the fact is that the opposite is true. Laura feels compelled to continue calling Sonja precisely because of Sonja's incessant complaining about her extended family; in Sonja's view they no longer care for her, if they ever had. In truth, all of Sonja's complaints are utterly baseless. The family does care very much about her, but Sonja's disrespectful criticism about everyone and everything has pushed her family members to distance themselves further and further away from Sonja. Regardless of the content of the conversation, the result is always the same; according to Sonja, Laura is to blame for her sibling's malicious disregard for Sonja, and Laura needs to take responsibility for fixing the situation.

Laura is in the 'no-win' middle. Every resolve Laura makes to herself to confront Sonja's behavior eventually dissolves into a personal <u>doubt</u> in herself. Laura always feels uncertain with Sonja, and with others as well. Laura wants to fix her sister, but even though she knows that Sonja suffers from a personality disorder, and is beyond any help that Laura could provide, Laura persists in her attempts, over and over, to 'make things all right.' It seems that Laura can't help herself; she is trapped in her <u>dependency</u> for approval, both from Sonja and everyone else. Laura seems unable to place any real confidence in her own beliefs. Exquisitely sensitive, Laura always defers her own needs and desires to those of others to the point where now she couldn't even remember her own genuine desires. Laura vacillates between <u>doubting</u> herself and over-<u>depending</u> on others. She is tired, confused, frustrated, and self-depreciating.

Laura's believing spiritual strength is <u>God Reliance</u>. She is a loyal and faithful person, perhaps not in a strict religious sense, but certainly in her everyday actions and friendships. She wants to rely on God fully but backs away from it because she both doubts herself and over-depends on others. This combination brings Laura only dismay and dissociation from her genuine self.

Laura needs to find her true center of <u>God Reliance</u>. She longs to align herself with the simple truth and power of God, not with the demands of the world and others. She needs to replace the erratic disharmony of her current style of living and find the peace at the center of her spiritual strength. Here is her power and her salvation from the haunting shadow of <u>doubt</u>, and the daunting excess of the compulsion of <u>dependency</u>.

2) Humility is ...

- Requiring very little to satisfy your ego needs
- Being free from affectation, free from playing roles
- Being free from projecting an image that is not genuinely you, free from wearing a mask or thick *persona*, free from putting on airs
- Being completely honest (but not brutally so) with yourself and with others
- Feeling free from worry and untainted by the cares of the world

The shadow of Humility is self-centeredness ...

1. Self-inflation, "puffing-up", being pert
2. Affecting mannerisms, egotism, over-opinion of oneself
3. Being overly forward, boastful
4. Self-love, putting on airs, or pretensions
5. Neglecting other's 'truth'
6. Conceit, complacency, exaggerated self-confidence
7. Projecting your 'truth' above all others
8. Rejecting other's 'truth'
9. Selfishness
10. Arrogance

The compulsion of Humility is self-abasement ...

1. Self-distrust
2. Fearing scrutiny of others
3. Excessive sense of inferiority, guilt, or shame
4. Closed to your own 'truth'

5. Over-reliance on the thoughts of others
6. Failure to recognize your strengths
7. Devalued opinion of own person and merits
8. Lack of faith in yourself
9. Neglectful of self ... self-reproach
10. Self-chastisement

Lack of Career Focus

Warren's Story

self-abasement <<<<< Humility >>>>> self-centeredness

Warren winced as he glanced at the alarm clock. In that instant, he could already hear his boss, and feel the ache in his stomach as he walked into work late yet again. *"How many times will it take before I learn my lesson,"* he thought as he lunged out of bed. His commute to work is saturated by a rising sense of guilt and an advancing inferiority. *"How stupid could I be?"* he keeps asking himself over and over. With each repetition he plunges deeper into <u>self-abasement</u>. That is Warren's pattern. He has lost count of the jobs he had forfeited in precisely this way. He is a good worker, he lacks no knowledge, talent, or skill to do the job well ... he simply lacks the drive. He starts every new job with enthusiasm, even gusto. Quickly however his motivation wanes and Warren confronts the same lack of faith in himself, the same fear of failure that had dismantled his resolve so many times before.

On a conscious level, Warren wants success. He dreams of owning his own company where he could really 'think big' and 'hit a homerun,' as he puts it. However, Warren secretly knows exactly how to engineer his own failure in ways that he could blame on others. His checkered work pattern has its effects not only on his career but also on his marriage. His wife empathizes with Warren's plight, but periodically her frustration bubbles over into anger. "*This isn't what I 'signed on for,*' she says. But each time she does so Warren counters with a monologue that begins as a contrite confession of his weaknesses, but quickly progresses into a litany of 'wrongs' he has encountered in his life: his domineering father, his 'preferred' brother, his injury that stopped his promising athletic career, his string of 'loser' bosses. His monologues always focus on him exclusively, and always have the same theme, Warren was the 'victim,' he had been wronged and slighted and sidestepped; he couldn't' get ahead because others just didn't understand. His reactions were always all about him, always <u>self-centered</u>. Concern for his wife, his children, his own responsibilities seems strangely absent.

Warren neglects the truth of the matter. He gives his self-defensive 'speeches' with a dramatic flair almost as if he enjoys them and has rehearsed them. Here he seems in his element, almost as though he has manufactured his career troubles just so he can plead his case in these paradoxically <u>self-depreciating</u> yet <u>self-centered</u> soliloquies. If his wife doesn't hold rapt attention, Warren raises his voice in anger, demanding her full concentration.

Warren broods and is filled with dread, and yet he can't face the truth that he sabotages his own success. In his heart, at his center, Warren actually wants very little; his ego needs are small. Unlike his father who achieved much, Warren seems to have made an internal commitment to himself that he would never be like his father. Where his father sought money and titles, Warren seeks only freedom from worries and release from responsibility. Yet, Warren can't confront this fact, he goes through the motions of trying to be like his father, but would invariably falter, only to resume the cycle over again. Warren's believing spiritual strength of humility becomes buried under a ruse, a pretense of incessant attempts at success, behavioral disguises hiding his real need for personal honesty … humility. Warren is caught in a vice between facing the guilt of pursuing his own desires, and the anger of pursuing the goals of others. This conundrum keeps Warren blind to himself and quite distant from his authentic self. Warren needs the power of honesty, the power of humility.

3) Acceptance is …

- Honoring the sense of being in accord with God
- Positively complying with God's truth
- Giving God your personal and complete "amen"
- Acknowledging God's ultimate authority
- Seeking alignment between your own will and God's will
- Letting go in trust
- Self-surrender without submission or resignation

The shadow of Acceptance is dissension

1. Emotional dis-ease
2. Discord or disagreement
3. Conflict seeking
4. Anger provocation

5. Clashing or working at cross-purposes
6. At issue with, at-odds, split
7. Breaking-off from
8. Enmity, division
9. Schism, break, at variance
10. Open hostility, warfare

The compulsion of Acceptance is aloofness ...

1. Harboring reserved and cool demeanor
2. Distancing oneself from situations, persons, and relationships
3. Withdrawal from others
4. Projecting a false sense of detachment from others
5. Cold shoulder, and passive aggressive avoidance
6. Setting oneself aside from, or above others
7. Removing self from mainstream of life
8. Denying reality
9. Avoiding by any means, including blaming
10. Blocking interactions, even through controlling behavior

Ovarian Cancer
Jill's Story

aloofness <<<<<<<<< Acceptance >>>>>>>>> dissension

As soon as Jill walked into my office I could see the emotional scars written all over her face that spoke of deep pain, physical, mental, and/or spiritual. The answer emerged almost immediately as Jill recounted her two year battle with ovarian cancer. Two years ago, at age 35, Jill had everything she thought she wanted, a big house, a wonderful husband and two fantastic children, and her own very successful company. One day a rare pain intensified forcing Jill to see a doctor. Two days later the diagnosis of a virulent ovarian cancer rocked her ordered life. Now, two years later, Jill wanted coaching on how to live her life optimally.

Toward the end of that first session, Jill said something I've never forgotten: *"All pain has purpose."* *"Wow,"* I said, *"that's a pretty pithy statement, what makes you say that so definitively?"* She responded, *"For months I experienced pain on so many levels, pain I thought I could conquer myself. But, the more I tried, the more it intensified. I'd never been up against anything like it before … I couldn't move it … I was powerless. My salvation was to begin living by a new standard, one that I formerly thought was only for losers … <u>acceptance</u>! Most people think of <u>acceptance</u> as submission or resignation, but it's neither. <u>Acceptance</u> is spiritual grit, it's giving up your own goals for higher ones, more real ones,"* she explained.

She confessed how she had first lapsed into <u>dissension</u>, feeling at odds with everything, angry with everybody; her life was marked by conflict and internal tension. The <u>dissension</u> waned and was replaced by a sense of wanting to be alone and aloof. She distancing herself from everyone, even her husband, she shut everyone out. She removed herself from life, withdrew from her friends and family. She adopted a flip attitude of disgust as she isolated herself. Yet, she explained, *"Some power overtook me, something bigger than me that taught me that I needed to change."*

She began faithful meditation, and she prayed, and she prayed some more. Slowly she dislodged from her anger and her <u>aloofness</u> and moved toward her personality center point. Gradually she acknowledged a higher calling in her cancer. She realized that she was beating the odds of survival, and realized further that her cancer must have a purpose. She began volunteering at the very hospital where she was treated, and by giving herself she found herself again. She knew that all sounded trite, but professed to its absolute truth. Jill had moved to <u>acceptance</u>, she had graduated to new levels of living unavailable to her when she was living her former life. *"Now,"* she said, *"I'm truly successful!"*

4) Mercy is ...

- Exercising leniency, forbearance, compassion, and true pity
- Being humane, tender, and empathic
- Exhibiting humanitarian action; justice
- Relenting ... letting go of judging, blaming, and the need to 'win'
- Granting clemency and forgiveness
- Giving to others ... sharing with those less fortunate

The shadow of Mercy is indifference ...

1. Bored, lazy, sluggish, uncaring
2. Being indecisive or half-hearted
3. Careless, insensitive, unobservant
4. Inattentive, without zest or zeal
5. Avoidant, inner criticism, unforgiving
6. Truculence, outrage, vent spleen
7. Malevolent, acrimony, hate
8. Malice, hard of heart, brutality
9. Inhumane, without humane feelings, non-lenient
10. Fierce, endangering health, cause mental suffering

The compulsion of Mercy is legalism …

1. Over-relying upon law and/or tradition
2. Seeking and quoting higher authority to excessive degree
3. Making self and others overly conform to standards
4. Imposing overly strict adherence to rules, laws, and regulations
5. Placing laws, standard procedures, regulations, etc. above human goodness
6. Over-zealous about order and control
7. Compelled to perform many good works
8. Hard-hearted, strict, demanding
9. Stubborn, stiff-necked, punitive
10. Immutable, condemning, harsh, unforgiving

Weight Management

Fran's Story

legalism <<<<<<<<<< Mercy >>>>>>>>> indifference

Fran put the peanut butter cup back into the candy dish and silently said to herself, *"I can be mercifully indifferent to that treat. That isn't a treat, it's a temptation."* Fran has a masterful grasp of her spiritual strengths; she is one of the few persons I know who has learned how to use her shadows and compulsions in service of her strengths. The notion of merciful indifference is counterintuitive. How can one be merciful and indifferent at the same time? Yet Fran's 'invention' is elegant in its operation for her weight management. Fran is an accomplished RN; she's made a lifelong study of diets and dieting motivated by her own weight battles, and has come to the conclusion that the success of a diet depends on how well one can tap into one's spiritual strengths. Fran even teaches her findings on diets and ideas about dieting in a very successful course she has developed based on the healing principles in this book. Fran is passionately dedicated to helping herself by helping others.

Fran attributes her weight management success to her believing spiritual strength of <u>mercy</u>. She says, *"If you want to be effective in dieting you must be affectively merciful toward yourself. You need to exercise all that is mercy: tenderness and compassion, forgiving, and always relenting."* Fran believes that diets are much too <u>legalistic</u>, *"They even label some foods as legal and others as illegal."* She abhors that type of thinking because it sets up a mentality of failure, and leads to the weight roller coaster ups and downs so common in strict dieting plans. Her weight management plan is deeper, it's not about food, *"Dieting is about living mercifully, it's about getting centered in your spirit, and it's about becoming rooted in your spiritual strengths."*

Fran preaches merciful <u>indifference</u> to her students, but is quick to add that <u>indifference</u> is not appropriate in other areas of life. One cannot be merciful indifferently to one's own needs, or family, or job, or dedication to one's life purpose. She says, *"I've been there, done that. I was indifferent to my own needs much too long and everybody suffered for it, my family, my job, but it was me who suffered most."* She points out how she was formerly insensitive to herself, inattentive and careless about the very core of her. She found herself avoiding others, being self-critical, and personally hard on herself. All that has changed since she's captured the true power of her personality … the power of <u>mercy</u>.

5) Hope is …

- Possessing the honest assurance that God is ultimately 'in charge'
- Conviction that love will remain the compelling force in life
- Recognizing the promise of ultimate fairness, goodness, and cheer
- Allowing yourself the perfect expectation that God's Will ultimately prevails
- Owning spiritual optimism and celestial confidence as your own

The shadow of Hope is despair …

1. Irritability, disillusionment
2. Being dreary, dull, and flat
3. Dispirited
4. Melancholy, sadness, and dismay
5. Heaviness, gloom, and weariness
6. Dejection, depression, oppressive emotional weight
7. Abject fatigue, severe guilt
8. Emptiness, alienation, weariness
9. Being broken hearted, and spiritless
10. Personal brokenness, hopelessness

The compulsion of Hope is presumption ...

1. Taking 'things' for granted
2. Emotional blindness
3. Knowing it all, or at least better than others
4. Projecting blame
5. Unrealistic permission to take liberties
6. An expectation of favored treatment
7. Assuming merit without appropriate work
8. A quality of personal entitlement
9. Assuming forgiveness without penance: impenitent
10. Absolving self from active participation in one's salvation

Drug Dependency

Joe's Story

presumption <<<<<<< Hope >>>>>>>>>> despair

It was 3 AM; Joe was in a downtown hotel room alone. His temples pulsated as he raised and finished his 20th beer. In six hours he'd be in front a panel of medical personnel with whom he'd worked for the last six months. They'd be making the final decision on a 6M-dollar surgical computer assemblage from a company that Joe represented. But tomorrow would wait, right now Joe's eyes were fixed on the movie on TV, and his mind was already floating in the anticipation of the next afternoon when he'd really get high.

Joe looked almost 'put together' as he ambled into the

conference room around 8:45 AM. A few eye drops temporarily cleared his vision, he only wished it could do the same for his head. One of Joe's problems was that he was so very good at what he did. He didn't even prepare any more; he'd fly into his presentations almost sleepwalking, bolstered by a <u>presumption</u> of success. He took for granted all his talent, all his knowledge, and all his accomplishment. He'd succeeded so many times before; this time would be the same.

The presentation was but a blur as he dropped off his rental car at the airport and boarded his plane. *"Double Scotch,"* he said to the flight attendant. By the time the plane landed he'd had three more rounds. Before he picked up his bags, he was on the phone to his supplier ordering his usual. He picked up the 'buy' and was back in a friend's apartment for the evening, fortified for a long and delightful night, but an agonizing next day.

Joe's life was unraveling. He was caught in the cycle of emotional 'downs' and chemical 'highs.' He'd move quickly now from disappointment, to disillusionment, to dread, to emptiness, and down to <u>despair</u>. The pattern always ended in drugs, with alcohol lubricating the gaps. Depression became Joe's constant companion, and chemicals were right along side.

Another hotel room, another binge, but this time something was different. The depression didn't lift, its heaviness pressed in on him and forced him out of his room and onto the interior balcony. Joe stared at the marble floor of the hotel lobby eight floors below; it looked so inviting … one move and his agony would be over. But some strength from his depths spoke to him, *"Joe, what about your children, what about your wife?"*

Somehow he pulled back from the railing and found himself on his knees in a cold shower. The next day he was mentally reeling at the stark ultimate failure he saw on that marble floor.

The image of the marble floor has never left Joe. He just celebrated his second anniversary of being clean and dry. He is a faithful AA participant, and trusted proponent and sponsor. He has a new job, and even though the faces are the same, he also has a new family. Joe has a new life … all based on the absolute assurance of the perennial power and might of God; a power that displays its potency daily through Joe's believing spiritual gift of <u>hope</u>.

Chapter Seven
Personality Function Two: Perceiving
The 'data' you focus on

Only rarely are you aware of your awareness. Your outlook on the world, and your insight into yourself is accomplished, for the most part, without the slightest recognition of what you're doing. Perceptions just seem to happen without any intention or volition on your part, yet how you frame or image what you encounter directs your life. What you choose to focus upon, and how you choose to frame it becomes your world; your perceptions make the world in which you live.

The perceiving function is perhaps the least understood of all six functions, like a mystery of unknowing, because most of us are blind to the process of awareness as it is unfolding. Your beliefs are like a magnet pulling you toward some images and away from others. Your premier perceiving spiritual strength draws you toward the Truth, while the shadow and compulsion of your perceiving premier strength pulls you toward unreality. It's only in reality where you can find healing. Healing calls you to an awareness of that which is beyond the material plane. Healing beckons you to stretch to a farther horizon of awareness, to see the divinity that is the driving force of your personality.

Events fill your life, and what you do first with these events, relationships, occurrences, or situations, emotional impressions, smells, tastes, panoramas, or whatever, before you do anything else, is *perceive* them. Your perceptions are as unique as your fingerprint; no one sees the world like you do because no one believes like you do. We do in fact have a personal point of view; actually we have many! Yet, the events of your life are essentially neutral, and all events are potentially helpful in that they have the power to teach us if we let them. Moving in this direction takes a steadfast resilience of purpose; a new vision of what is reality. If you don't see reality, you see only illusion. Healing means raising your vision beyond the illusion that the shadows and compulsions show you as illness, and rising above the problems of the material plane.

All those beliefs, attitudes, and values you have stored in your belief core (the first function of your personality) begin their intense influence over your personality when you progress to the second function of your personality ... your perceiving function. The perceiving function gathers data from all around you as well as inside you. Dr. Deepak Chopra, physicist, medical doctor, and popular author says that we summon forth the kind of data that reinforces our belief paradigm. Your data gathering mechanisms, or sensate mechanisms, are constantly scanning the horizon of your exterior and interior worlds searching for whatever is of interest to your beliefs.

What interests your ego most falls into two categories: 1) what agrees with or confirms your beliefs, and 2) what contradicts your beliefs. Yet, to discover the healing strength within, you need to see with new eyes, the eyes of your True Self, which focuses on something different. Your True Self focuses only on the true reality of what's presented to you … the reality of Universal Love, here is where healing lies. When you look only for what you agree with, you activate your shadows, and when you focus on what you don't agree with, you activate your compulsions. You can train your sensate mechanisms to focus on whatever you direct: 1) true reality, 2) only what you agree with, or 3) only what you disagree with; the choice is always yours.

Anthony DeMello, Jesuit priest and author, devoted his entire apostolic adult life to perception. In all of his writing and all of his speaking he never tired of asking the same question to his readers and audiences: *"Are you sure you're awake? How do you know you're awake? How do you know you're not simply sleepwalking through life?* These are pretty pithy questions that speak to what he called awareness. Of what are you aware? Where is the center of your awareness? To what do you give illumination?

You need to see yourself differently, not as a depository of problems, but as a container of divinity, a powerful spiritual well of healing energy that is waiting to be dipped. You need to see yourself as part of the cosmic energy field that emanates from the first source and center of all energy … God. To accomplish this you can step back from your normal perceptions, how you usually see things, and take a longer view of what's actually going on in your personality. Who is in-charge of your perceptions? Have you put your spiritual strength in charge, or the shadows and compulsions? Don't focus on what's not there, what's missing, instead focus only on the absolute reality of the universe ... Universal Love, from which your spiritual strength flows. When you move in this direction, you move toward your spiritual strength; you move toward healing.

All events are neutral until you put your perceiving function to work on them, then they change to conform to your beliefs. Suppose you saw a close-up picture of a Neanderthal caveman holding a knobby club above his head. You notice that his face is contorted, his nostrils are flared, his eyebrows pursed, and his teeth gritted. Your sensory impression of this picture is of a very angry man. Now the picture widens and you see that this man is guarding the front of a cave where his family is huddled in fright of the saber toothed tiger snarling right in front of the cave. Now your sensory impression changes, no longer do you see an angry man, instead you see a brave man. Even though the caveman's facial expression hasn't changed, what you see has changed. Because you see more data, you perceive the same picture differently.

You do have the power to change your perception anytime you want. Dr. Gerald Jampolsky, M.D., a psychiatrist and author from the San Francisco Bay area, has a favorite saying that he uses whenever he's feeling low, sad, sour, or just plain out-of-sorts: "*I could see this differently*." When you change your perception, the way you see things, you automatically change your world. By changing your perception you literally change the reality right in front of you.

How do we know that our perceptions of reality are accurate? That's hard. Sometimes we need to heal our misperceptions but we don't even know we're misperceiving. We can suffer from 'partial vision,' like looking through a knothole in the fence at the ballpark but making judgments on the entire game. How do we move to 'wholeness vision,' where we see the broader horizon and consequently perceive more accurately? How can we change our faulty vision, false perception, and distorted perception? Might this have something to do with our spiritual strengths?

Whatever problem you think you perceive may not be the actual problem at all, perhaps the problem is in your basic outlook or insight. Some people see what we used to call a juvenile delinquent and want to build more prisons, others see the same young man and want to change the justice system. Both people see a problem, but the problem they see is very different; of course, they both believe their beliefs are correct. Chances are that their solutions to the problem will be very different as well. Isn't it like this with most things? Again, our perceptions are as unique as our fingerprint.

> The optimist looks at an oyster and expects to see a pearl; the pessimist looks at the same oyster and expects ptomaine poisoning. The optimist sees an opportunity in every calamity, while the pessimist sees the opposite.

Jonathan Edwards, the revered and also hated (depending on your perception) Puritan minister of the 18th century, once said something quite profound about our perceiving function: *"Saints do not see things others do not see. On the contrary, they see just what everyone else sees – but they see it differently."* So, it may not be what you focus on, but how you perceive it that makes a grand difference in the way you live your life. Could you train yourself to perceive all the events that come along in your life as instructive lessons … as teachers?

I'm not a Japanese Haiku poetry expert, not by any stretch, but I did hear an interview with a real Haiku expert on the radio one day. When asked by the commentator if he could recite his favorite Haiku poem, he immediately launched into this one:

While visiting Kyoto and the cuckoos,
I found myself longing
For Kyoto and the cuckoos.

At first I thought the man was joking, but upon closer investigation I came to perceive this poem as saying something profound about perception. Kyoto is considered a holy city in Japan, and a visit to the city during the two times of the year when the cuckoo birds migrate through is considered especially so. The author of the poem was obviously making a return trip to Kyoto when he perceived that his internal reaction to the event was not of the same quality as what he had experienced on his first visit to the city during cuckoo migration time. He was so struck by this sensation that he wrote this poem.

We wrap up bunches of singular perceptions into little bundles that we squirrel away in our memories and call these bundles our experience. Have you ever started a sentence with, *"From my experience."*? What you were saying was something like, *"Here's my overall impression of this subject that I've amalgamated from all my little perceptions about it."*

Some years ago I learned a lesson in perceiving. I came home from work to find that my wife had wall papered the bathroom. I remember complimenting her on her quick and stealthy work, since her work was a surprise to me. The next morning while shaving in front of the bathroom mirror, I noticed that there was an overlapping seam in the wallpaper right at my eye level.

I looked at the seam with a scowl; I saw the seam as a flaw in her work and something of a failure on her part. The next day I had a similar perception with its attendant thoughts and feelings. This was followed by the same perception on the third day. On the fourth day I became weary of my perception of her 'flaw" and decided to "see this differently." Was my wife lazy? No! Was my wife careless? No! Was my wife intentionally trying to ruin my day? Certainly not! Well, what was my wife? My wife is parsimonious; she routinely goes out of her way to 'catch a bargain." My wife's attitude is a behavioral result of growing up in family that was, but didn't know that it was, poor. She would not buy another double roll of wallpaper just to avoid a seam; this would have violated her basic value system and a denigration of her belief core. We've since moved, but for the rest of my days in that house, I made a point of looking at that seam every morning and perceiving a beautiful aspect of the wonderful woman I married. I could see it differently once my vision morphed to wholeness. I've never forgotten the lesson in right perception.

You've probably heard the old story of the three bricklayers; I repeat it here because it points up yet another aspect of the perceiving function of your personality. The first was asked what he was doing and replied, *"I'm laying bricks!"* The second bricklayer answered the same question with, *"I'm building a cathedral."* The third one answered, *"I'm helping to bring heaven on earth!"* Yes, it is all in your perception. By the way, what are you doing?

Other words that speak to the perceiving function are: Imagination, dreams and daydreams, insight and outlook, illusions and delusions, point of view, memories, observances, visions, reflections, visualize, and "in your mind's eye."

Psychiatrist R. D. Lang wrote a most creative poem about perception.

The Mind's Denial Reflex

> The range of what we think and do
> is limited by what we fail to notice.
> And because we fail to notice
> that we fail to notice,
> there is little we can do
> to change
> until we notice
> how failing to notice
> shapes our thoughts and deeds.

Spiritual Strengths and Accurate Perceiving

Your perceiving spiritual strength is the guiding power leading you to 'right' or accurate and healing perceiving. Always consult this energy as you assess the validity of your perceptions of anything and anyone. Here is your guide, your perceiving coach, who gently opens your eyes to the truth of what's right in front of you. You must look inside yourself for the guidance to see accurately. When you look only outside yourself for answers, you distort your perceptions by locking them on the level of form, the level of the material; you're seeing only what, and as, the world sees.

To perceive accurately you're called to tap into energy beyond this world, an energy that comes not from the shrill siren song of the *ego*, but from a cosmic melody of grace gently guiding you to the truth. This universal energy within you expands your perception to the boundaries of true awareness: true self-awareness and true other-awareness. As you gradually move in this direction you begin to feel a new zest for life, enriched relationships, and most of all, a new peace of heart that's beyond any former vision.

When you call upon your perceiving spiritual strength you open yourself to a new energy source and move away from the dysenergy in your perceiving shadow and compulsion. Dysenergy robs you of your true potentials, the purpose for which you came here. This energy allows you to perceive the real you, not some facsimile of you that your ego is 'selling.' You are not what the world says you are, you are far more than the occupational roles you perform on this planet. You are essentially a packet of divine cosmic energy, connected to all energy in ways we do not yet understand. Your true reality is well beyond what you can see with your eyes, well beyond even what you can think. Your perceiving strength offers you a glimpse into this infinite potential that you are, and gives you the necessary power to bring this potential into reality. Your interior celestial healing coach speaks to you daily about the vastness of your potentials; your perceiving strength allows you to listen carefully.

Chapter Eight

The Five Spiritual Strengths, Shadows, and Compulsions Of the Perceiving Function of the Personality

Here are the five spiritual strengths of the perceiving function of the personality, along with their corresponding shadows and compulsions. One of these strengths is your premier strength, the guiding strength of your perceiving function. You identified your premier perceiving strength when you took the *Spiritual Strengths Finder*. Of course, you're also most vulnerable to the shadow and compulsion that stand as foreboding anti-energies on either side of your premier strength.

Compulsion …..Spiritual Strength ……..Shadow

illusion <<<<<<<<< Vision >>>>>>>>blindedness

recklessness <<<<<< Humor >>>>>>>>lamentation

appeasement <<<<< Peace >>>>>>>>>>contention

self-forfeiture <<<< Adaptability >>>>>> rigidity

bluntedness <<<<<< Simplicity >>>>>>> complexity

6. Vision is …

- Seeing the world through the eyes of God
- Possessing the clear awareness that there is another realm beyond the physical
- The ability to catch a glimpse of the eternal here on earth
- The power to discern the hand of God in the events of your life
- View the 'light of the eternal' shining behind the actions of human kind

The shadow of vision is <u>blindedness.</u>

1. Focused solely on the five physical senses
2. Limited perception
3. Seeing things or people inaccurately
4. Not seeing the whole picture
5. Failure to focus
6. Lack of awareness
7. Dim-sighted, groping in the dark
8. Unsighted because of ambition or pain
9. Sightlessness, closed, undiscerning
10. Hiding the eternal truth

The compulsion of vision is <u>illusion</u>

1. That which precludes true wisdom
2. Seeing what is not there, not real
3. Sensing nothing as something, or vice versa
4. Discerning meaning where none exists
5. Failing to see true meaning

6. Failing to see what is reality
7. Misinterpret, masking the real, deforming
8. Deception or confusion
9. Engaging in images that are unreal
10. Living a life of fantasy

Family Disharmony
John's Blindedness

John shuddered as he related how his oldest son had once again been arrested for possession of drugs. Sullen, yet intensely angry, John simply threw up his hands in disgust and then slowly pulled them back down burying his face in shame. *"How could this be?"* he muttered. This was the third time John's son had been arrested; the first was when he was only 17. For five years John has lived in his shadow of <u>blindedness</u> and his compulsion of <u>illusion</u>. Today, perhaps for the first time, John is inching toward his strength of <u>Vision</u>. John could no longer block the searing reality that his son was addicted to drugs, that his world was in pieces because of drugs, and that until he sought treatment, his life would continue to spin out of control.

John foundered in a sea of denial only infrequently breaking the surface to view the truth of his son's life … and his own. John was a good father, perhaps too good, if that's possible. Too good in that John always demanded the absolute best from his son; John never missed an opportunity to "teach" his son about what he had just done wrong, or to avoid doing wrong. John wanted perfection. Certainly John would never admit that, no, he would always say things like *"Boys will be boys!"* and other similar adages. But John's behavior didn't lie; he wanted and expected perfection from his son.

John was a man of regularity, even habituation. Every moment of every day, John had well planned; each day was essentially a repeat of the day before ... that's the way John lived his life. Without being aware of it, John had lapsed into a kind of sleep walking state of existence. Strangely, John was rewarded and even lauded for his worldview. John referred to himself as a "simple" man, but in reality, John wasn't simple, he was simplistic. He couldn't or didn't reflect on the meaning of life, the deeper values of life; John's perception was stuck in a two-dimensional view of living that blocked him from truly connecting with his son, and kept him in the dark as to the truth of what was happening to his son. In John's mind, he had done all he could do to make his son the best man ever; he couldn't' see that all his teaching was actually critical and condescending, preaching and damaging to his son's development. John was blind, and was only now realizing just how sightless he had been.

Over time, John was able to grab onto his spiritual strength of Vision, and realize his own perceptual stubbornness over the years. Vision gave him new eyes to see himself and his son with a new clarity, a celestial clarity that transcended the worldly horizon of his past. John eventually came to realize that he needed to look through a new set of eyes, eyes that were compassionate yet firm, sensitive yet courageous, and caring yet disciplined. John did learn to let his gift of Vision lead him out of his bleak life landscape. Here was his healing.

7. Humor is …

- Discovering, expressing, or appreciating the ludicrous or absurdly incongruous
- Finding comical or amusing cheer in the human condition
- Finding levity in oneself by taking a completely objective viewpoint
- Recognizing the light side, seeing delight, exultation, revelry, and jubilation
- Being optimistic and sparkling
- To appreciate self as God does

The shadow of humor is <u>lamentation</u>

1. Inability to laugh at foibles
2. Feeling insulted when challenged
3. Taking on a helpless frame of mind
4. Making oneself a victim
5. Self pity, woe is me
6. To whine, moan, or grumble ceaselessly
7. To complain and criticize without cause
8. Chronically angry
9. To hold a grudge
10. Loss of hope

The compulsion of humor is <u>recklessness</u>

1. Hiding behind a laugh
2. To make fun of, or to cover-up a situation
3. Making a joke to avoid something important
4. Holding a hurt with a tight-lipped smile

5. Affectionate teasing with a 'bite'
6. To laugh at or make fun of others
7. To insult in light-hearted manner
8. Poke fun at another's expense
9. To attack or belittle in false humor
10. Mocking or ridiculing self or others in 'fun'

Low Self-Esteem
Harry's Recklessness

Harry slapped his knee as he let out a robust guffaw. Harry was a master at getting people to laugh; his own smile and face-contorting laugh pulled nearly everyone into his world of levity. Quick of mind, and easy with words, Harry could take control of every social situation and transform it into a playful exhibition of mirth. People loved Harry; he truly was the life of the party. Inviting Harry to a house gathering insured it would become a riot of laughter. Harry was the jester; he "held court" with his quips, jokes, teases, flashing hand and body movements, and never-ending flow of laughs, laughs, and more laughs. Yet there was so much more to Harry than laughs.

Harry deftly uses his <u>humor</u> in a <u>reckless</u> manner. He contorts his <u>humor</u> to hide his pain, his insecurity, and his guilt. Harry is truly a good man, yet as adept as he appears to be at connecting with others, his reality is quite the opposite. He hides behind his <u>humor,</u> uses it to deflect, defer, or otherwise avoid his internal pain. Harry's <u>humor</u> is his armor protecting him from having to face his terrible view of himself, a view that casts him as a 'loser,' as one 'not worthy,' as a 'fake.' Paradoxically Harry fakes his behavior, so as to hide his perception of himself as a fake. Harry's <u>humor</u> works so well for him, that he is never trapped by an awkward question, he can always deflect an inquiry into his personal life with a joke or humorous distraction that never fails to bring a laugh. He perverts his spiritual strength of humor into a life avoidance vehicle instead of the life strengthening power it actually is.

Underneath Harry's constant humor lies sadness, a pain of self-rejection so large and so ugly that he has to hide it at all costs. Over the years Harry has adopted this perverted <u>humor</u> as his standardized persona or mask; a mask that lay on his nightstand where it rests until Harry puts it back on each morning. Harry's mask hides his shadow of his humor … <u>lamentation</u>. Harry is the proverbial class clown, laughing on the outside and crying on the inside.

The day that Harry realized (perceived) that others might actually be able to see through his mask of perverted <u>humor,</u> was the very day that he began to pull out of his arrested emotional and spiritual growth. Harry rose to see two new things: 1) he was not the 'bad guy' that he thought he was, and 2) people loved him even without his armor of <u>humor</u>. Harry entered his sixth decade of life with new eyes able to see in a new light. <u>Humor</u> was his gift, his strength, and his friend, he didn't have to abuse it any longer, he was now free to find the true <u>humor</u> in life … he learned to laugh internally at the role of 'fool' that he had played for so long. This alone gave Harry a new peace of mind and a new view of himself. Here was Harry's healing.

8. Peace is …

- Listening to the great quiet within
- Finding harmony and concord in virtually everything you encounter
- Knowing you live in celestial security and serenity
- Living in a state where love abides
- The gift of tranquility you receive when a higher plan for your happiness emerges, one that you didn't see

The shadow of peace is <u>contention</u>

1. Being defensive
2. To become easily upset
3. To be chronically unfriendly
4. To be oppositional, contrary
5. Quickly move to anger
6. To be destructive for no cause
7. To be unnecessarily suspicious
8. To oppose, to pick a fight
9. To confront, contest, debate, or duel
10. To provoke or create controversy without cause

The compulsion of peace is <u>appeasement</u>

1. Avoidance of personal responsibility
2. To soothe so as to gain favor with another
3. To falsely apologize
4. Overly promising
5. To atone for unnecessarily
6. To placate by avoiding the real issue at hand
7. To pacify, give others what they want without cause

8. To move to peace at any price
9. To mollify
10. Abandon one's true needs

---<<<>>>---

Fear of Abandonment
Sally's Contention

Sally dug her fingernails into her palms as she related yet another story about a friend that she felt had betrayed her again. *"This always happens to me. Why do I let it happen over and over?"* she lamented. When her spiritual counselor asked Sally what she wanted to do about this situation, Sally hung her head and said, *"I can't confront my friend! What will she think of me?"* Once again Sally retreated into her compulsion of appeasement; she feigned peace, pretended that everything was all right; that no infraction had occurred … everything was fine. But of course, everything was not fine inside of Sally. She was anxious, tense, scared, full of fear of abandonment, and an intense sense of self-depreciation.

Here was Sally's trap. She projects only the appearance of peace, of everything being fine, only to cover-up the reality that she is full of contention inside.

Sally's shadow of contention shows up in ways not very obvious. She gossips, and plants seeds of doubt in other's minds, all the while playing the role of victim. Without even being aware of it, Sally 'stirs the pot' in any social or family situation. She unconsciously pits one person against another, playing the game "Let's you and you fight." Sally is very good at this, it gives her some sense of power over others and alleviates her own intense sense of powerlessness, if only temporarily. Sally manipulates the situation to appear that she is the innocent bystander who is only trying to help others, when actually she is agitating others to anger. In some paradoxical way, Sally's actions salve her own internal anger. Once she is successful at causing a disagreement, she always offers the false palm branch of appeasement, disguised as peace. Naturally she has the power of peace within her, but she equivocates between causing contention, and appeasing; she waffles between her shadow and compulsion.

It was only when this unknowing psycho-emotional 'scam' was unveiled by her spiritual counselor that Sally began her journey to true peace in her soul. It took several years for her to unlearn her past practices, and take-on the healthy power of 'listening to the great quiet within.' Here was Sally's healing.

9. Adaptability is ...

- To be flexible, the ability to shift one's view at one's own volition
- To be selfless while retaining selfhood
- Conforming to spiritual growth
- To adopt the will of Universal Love above one's own
- Converting yourself from the separation the world teaches to the unity that Universal Love teaches
- Adjusting to being in this world and also not of it at the same time

The shadow of adaptability is <u>rigidity</u>

1. Threatened by change
2. Doubt views of others have any truth
3. Critical and judging
4. Perceptually congealed
5. Disrespectful of point of view of others
6. Concretize your own point of view
7. Immobile, non-flexible, stiff, stagnant
8. Sticking to the letter, and not the spirit of the law
9. Being tight and/or forceful
10. Overly strict or harsh

The compulsion of adaptability is <u>self-forfeiture</u>

1. Chronically hyper-alert to the needs of others at the expense of your own
2. Inability to say 'no'
3. Always being the 'helper on call'
4. Giving-up your sense of self-direction
5. Obsequious
6. Negating your own needs, desires, and goals
7. Doubting or denying your views
8. Lack of trust of your perspective
9. Failure to be true to self
10. Giving away your integrity

---<<<>>>---

Marriage 'On the Rocks'
Tracey's Rigidity

Tracey exploded at her husband of only three months in an avalanche of verbal attack. When exhausted she backed away from him and wondered aloud why she had married him. Right at this moment he appeared harsh, forceful, inflexible, critical, narrow-minded, and certainly disrespectful of her wishes. These were all the personal traits that she abhorred more than any others ... all the traits that her own ego threw up to her in her shadow of <u>rigidity</u>. All she could say was, *"What have I done in marrying you?" "How can I get out of here?"* Her shadow of <u>rigidity</u> forced her to see only bad, it inflated small imperfections into gigantic transgressions, it projected all of her own fears about herself onto her husband who stood before Tracey dumbfounded at his wife's uncharacteristic behavior.

Tracey tried to be the perfect wife. She seemed to never tire of giving of herself. She appeared three steps ahead of her husband around the house, endlessly dusting, cleaning, straightening, tidying, and so forth. Somehow asking her husband for help, or even expecting his assistance invaded some place of duty within her. Tracey was supposed to be all things to all people; she gave, gave, and gave some more. Yet all her helping always generated in her to a sense that she was being discounted, overlooked, and even dismissed. Her giving was her way of requesting attention, being noticed, seeking applause, grasping for a sense of integrity. But it was a false integrity, a fraudulent internal cohesion that always boomeranged into the same sense of <u>self-forfeiture</u>, self-depreciation, being unappreciated and discounted.

Here was her contorted way of trying to express her spiritual strength of adaptability, overindulge others with doing, so she would feel accepted. Tracey was stuck in her shadow of <u>rigidity</u>. She couldn't see that her attempts were causing the opposite of what she wanted. She couldn't move to a new perceptual 'place.' In her unexamined mind she thought that if she were to change (become <u>adaptable</u>) that she would somehow lose the only way she knew to gain self-appreciation … a sense of being OK.

Letting-go of her <u>rigidity</u> was the hardest thing she had to do. It wasn't until her marriage was threatened by her now frequent anger outbursts at her husband, that she was able to confront her own shadows and compulsions that had trapped her into a dismal view of herself and of her place in the world. She began to 'get in touch' with her beautiful spiritual strength of <u>adaptability</u>. She learned that she could be her true self AND be adaptable at the same time; indeed, she learned that unless she acted with a true spirit of <u>adaptability</u> that honored her own needs as well as the needs of others. Here was her healing.

10. Simplicity is …

- Being exquisitely open and child-like
- Possessing a naïve gracefulness, loveliness, and charm
- Having the qualities of radiance and magnificence
- Having no pretense, being uncomplicated and innocent
- Something or someone that brings pleasure that clean, delicate, elegant, and glorious
- Seeking the goodness in everyone

The shadow of simplicity is <u>complexity</u>

1. Accepting information overload
2. Pressured, divided, de-energized
3. Clouded, scattered, confused
4. Disorganized or sluggish perception
5. Being complicating, entangled,
6. Disturbed and distorted perception
7. Information paralysis
8. Fragmented, disintegrated, immobile
9. Seeing no purpose in life/ overly identified with the world
10. Cataclysmic perceptual failure

The compulsion of simplicity is <u>bluntedness</u>

1. Oversimplification
2. Finding it easy to give insensitive and quick 'labels'
3. Being insensitive and rough to self and others
4. Painfully simplistic, failure to work through details
5. Mindlessly simplistic
6. Prejudices honored as 'truth'
7. Unyielding and immoveable
8. Toxic oversimplification and irreverence
9. Dysfunctional simplicity
10. Prejudices dominate perception

---<<<>>>---

Lack of Focus
Fred's Creative Simplicity

As a successful artist, Fred's work is anything but simple. His abstract impressionism oils and acrylics are perhaps overly complex in terms of color, form, space, and movement. However, under all the complexity is the simple fact that Fred loves what he does. He revels in the simple grace he's received to be an artist in the form that he loves best. There are moments in the creative process when Fred enters a trance-like state and feels completely open, not just to the intrinsic process as it regards art, but to the panorama of art as a spiritual experience. Fred sometimes senses another dimension going on around him, engulfing him. At such times he has the idea that heaven is not 'out there' but is another dimension surrounding him, and all of us, all the time. In the creative process, the intuitive process, Fred taps into this dimension. This only happens when Fred gives himself over fully to the art.

When Fred allows his compulsion of complexity to enter the picture, such as watching too much TV, or reading too many mysteries, he notices that his spiritual strength languishes. Sometimes his strength of simplicity can seem to vanish. Once it's gone, it takes a long time of intense studio work to get it back. The complexity enters when Fred gives himself over to busyness and unnecessary work. At such times he feels disorganized, mentally scattered, perceptually stalled, and physically fatigued. As an artist, Fred needs to be emotionally and physically centered, he needs to be 'on task' but not overly so. When Fred forces concentration he notices that he reverts back to complexity, and feels pressured and distorted. When this happens he can easily slip into his compulsion of

<u>bluntedness</u>.

When 'off center' Fred notices that he can become 'short' with his wife. At such times he finds it all too easy to be critical; he can take verbal swipes at himself, at his wife, and even at God. He makes sweeping over-generalized assessments (criticisms) about a person, or situation, the government, his church, anything, on only the smallest bites of information. He views the world through a very narrow knothole in the fence and makes sweeping and negative evaluations about the whole.

Fred has learned to re-grip himself at such times, by first realizing the dismal view he's taking about things, stepping back from himself, and looking anew, with new eyes. He internally repeats, *"I could see this differently."* He can reconnect with his wonderful spiritual strength of <u>simplicity</u> and once again see things clearly. Here is Fred's healing.

Chapter Nine
Personality Function Three: Thinking
How your personality makes meaning

There is nothing either good or bad, but thinking makes it so.
William Shakespeare

Thoughts are your internal communications; thoughts are what you say to yourself. Imagine that you're driving on the freeway in rush hour traffic. Its' cold, in fact, it's sleeting. You're headed for a job interview that you've labored hard to get, when suddenly you hear a muffled thud, and notice that it's hard to steer. You manage to squeeze over through traffic and snug up to the guardrail. How many thoughts rocket through your mind from the time you first hear the thud, get out of your car, feel the stinging sleet on your neck, almost get hit by other cars, realize your new suit is getting ruined, and finally see your flat tire?

Thoughts are your almost automatic internal communications; they're like hundreds or thousands of internal emails flying around your mind at the same time each carrying bits of data. Some of these emails come from your perceiving function with data from the outside world, while others are internally produced by your thinking function. Through all this SPAM it's hard to make sense of what's really going on and how to make sense of it. You need a good SPAM filter.

You're thinking all the time, and the vast majority of that time you're quite unaware of what you're thinking. All these ideas are racing around your mind, each one charged with energy, and you're oblivious to almost all of them. Some words that might help you better grasp the ubiquitous nature of your thoughts are: interpretations, evaluations, judgments, understandings, criticisms, enlightenments, reflect upon, consider, deliberate, contemplate, meditate, ponder, study, weigh, collect your thoughts, turn over in your mind, bear in mind, reconsider, cross your mind, engrossed in thought, all things considered, train of thought, flow of ideas, and assessments.

Who is in-charge?

What, or who is in-charge of the thinking function of your personality? You say that you are, but, which you? When you change your mind, who is making the change? At whose authority are you making this mind change, is it your true self or your false self? Spiritual philosopher Thomas Merton asked the same question; he devoted much of his time and a lot of ink trying to describe the distinction between the two selves.

False self: the external and superficial self, the shadow self, the petty self, the ego self, the manipulative self, the protective self, the alien self, the frightened self, the false success self, and many more.

True self: the inner and hidden self, the creative and mysterious inmost self, the deepest self, the awakened self, the illuminated self, the self perfectly at peace, the knowing self, the self of the cosmos, and more.

What might be some differences between the thoughts created by the false self (ego) and those created by the real self? Thoughts from the false self are fundamentally self-protective. We, of course, need protection, yet if our ego self is over-emphasized simple self-protection can easily become exaggerated into more malevolent thinking: judging, criticism, worldliness, self-serving, reactive, hurtful, inaccurate, separated, contentious, prejudicial, and manipulative. Thoughts like these distortions of thinking create distance between people; they make us skeptical, suspicious, and even paranoid.

Thoughts originating from the real self are fundamentally loving and compassionate: peaceful, affirming, untroubled, secure, silent, sometimes spiritual and prayerful, considerate, compassionate, personal, reflective, and the like. Thoughts originating from your true self create harmony and unity; they encourage understanding, forgiveness, moderation, healing, and peace.

All the way through our formative years, and indeed into our early adult years, the 'thought system' of the ego self generally takes the leadership position in the personality. But usually in the middle years we gradually pass the 'torch' of leadership from our ego self to our real self. As this happens a new 'thought system' gradually emerges that shifts how we make sense of our experiences. We let go of thinking only as the world thinks, and can move to a more transcendent plane. St. Paul puts this very well when he says; "*I now walk more by faith and less by sight.*"

Which self do you want 'in charge' of your personality thinking function?

There's no either-or answer to this question. A better question might be, what percentage of your thoughts is created by your ego self, and what percentage comes from your true self? What percentage of your thoughts are judgmental, or 'fear' thoughts, that bring you blame, criticism, and condemnation, and what percentage are helping, or 'Universal Love' thoughts that bring you harmony, learning, forgiveness, understanding, and the like? There are no neutral thoughts; your thoughts either affirm you or others, or they condemn you or others. Healing requires that you turn-off our false self (ego) and place your thoughts at the direction of your true self.

If you can't change it, change the way you think about it

The role of counseling and therapy is to help you live a more effective and personally satisfying life; consequently counseling is about change. Interestingly, most people arrive in my counseling office with an assumption that other people need to change: my husband, my boss, my kids, my mother, even the world. Gradually, and often times reluctantly, they realize that the change needs to occur in them first. Psychology has a name for this phenomenon; we call this the 'elegant solution,' real change happens inside, not outside of us. The fact is that as you meander through your life you need to change your mind! Changing your mind means that you need to change your thoughts … change your thinking.

Thoughts possess dynamic power and energy. The so –called law of expectation asserts that things seem to turn out pretty much the way we thought they would. The new medical discipline of *psychoneuroimmunology* studies the interactions between your mind (psycho), your central nervous system (neuro), and your immune system. Primarily, psychoneuroimmunology looks at the role of your thinking on your health. Do you think you can think yourself sick? When I was in grade school, there were many mornings when I was pretty sure that I was very sick to my stomach; at least until my mother relented and said I could stay home from school. Many therapies, especially group counseling, seek healing simply by allowing participants to express their deepest thoughts. We really don't know why, and certainly not how it works!

There are no idle thoughts. All thoughts seek form; all thoughts seek expression. Wayne Dyer says it another way, when he says, *"You become what you think about all day long."*

World 'social thought raiser' Peace Pilgrim, a very illuminated, and dedicated social worker who helped displaced Europeans dig their way out of the aftermath of World War II, had this to say about thoughts: *"If you realized how powerful your thoughts are … you would never think a negative thought!"*

William James, known as the father of American psychology, said, *"The greatest discovery of my generation is that human beings can alter their lives by altering their minds."*

Christian scripture has a similar 'take' on thinking. *"Be ye transformed by the renewing our your mind."* St. Paul's letter to the Romans 12, 1-2.

What we think about always expands in our thinking function. You can think of your thoughts as actual things, physical objects that you can actually observe from a distance. Just observing your thoughts will slow down your mind and bring you to that still point within where you will find peace.

Positive vs. negative thinking

Negative thinking means that we are somehow distorting reality … thinking inaccurately. Here are 15 different ways we can "do" negative thinking.

The 15 Thought Distortions

    1)   <u>Knotholing</u>: People who knothole consider only a very

small part of a very large situation and pass judgment on the entire situation based on the small part alone. People who do this often operate with insufficient evidence and/or knowledge. Examples: *"People are so stupid!* or, *"I'm worthless, I can't do anything right!"*

2) Polarizing: Those who polarize think of all people, events, situations, and so forth, as fitting into two neat categories –good and bad. Variations on this polarized theme might be wonderful versus terrible, excellent versus no good, up versus down, "for me" versus "against me," and so on. Examples: *"All politicians are crooks."* Or *"All doctors have perfect knowledge on how to treat patients."* Or *"When I get A's, I know I'm brilliant. When I get B's, I know I'm stupid."*

3) Forecasting: When people forecast, they make judgments about the future based only on hunches, intuitions, superstitions, vague feelings, or wild assumptions alone. Two subcategories of forecasting are mind reading and fortune telling. Example: *"Guess what he's going to do next; he always does it,"* or, *"You know how she thinks; she's just like that,"* or, *"I know I'll fail. I always fail at this."*

4) Doomsaying: When people immediately jump to the worst possible consequences in any situation, event, or relationship, they are doomsaying. Example: *"Oh no, it's starting to rain. We'll have a tornado!"* or, *"That girl I spoke with yesterday didn't even look at me today. I know she hates me now that she knows what I'm really like."*

5) Self-Blaming: When people blame themselves, they interpret everything bad that happens as being in some

way their own fault Examples: *"Mary seems unhappy today. I must have hurt her,"* or, *"I can't make a speech like Richard. There must be something wrong with me."*

6) <u>Controlling:</u> When people think in a controlling fashion, they conclude that they are responsible for everything that happens to them. Examples: *"Without me they won't be able to do anything,"* or, *"If only I'd been prettier, my father would have liked me better than my sister."*

7) <u>Victimizing:</u> When people think like victims, they assume that they are controlled by forces outside themselves, or beyond their control. Examples: *"There is something in me that just stops me every time I try that,"* or, *"My parents didn't raise me right. That's why I have so many problems now."*

8) <u>Idealizing:</u> When people idealize, they think that there is always a right or fair way of doing something. They think that all things should always be fair, and all people should be fair. Examples: *"Are you sure you are doing that right?"* or, *"It's only fair; if I wash his clothes, he should take me out to dinner."*

9) <u>Emotionalizing:</u> When people emotionalize, they think only based on the way they feel. Examples: *"I just know she's out to trap me. I can feel it,"* or, *"I sometimes feel so stupid, so it must be so."*

10) <u>Adjusting:</u> When people assume that other persons or things must change or adjust to suit their own belief core, they are exhibiting the distortion called adjusting. Examples: *"Why are you so spineless? You need to have more self-discipline,"* or, *"To my way of thinking, if those people on welfare can't do better than that, then*

they deserve to live in the decrepit conditions they're in."

11) <u>Labeling:</u> When people label, they like to categorize and attach names or attributes to others based on incomplete evidence. Examples: *"All people from the South are slow,"* or, *"He didn't like me; I must be a real dud."*

12) <u>Projecting:</u> When people project, they blame something or someone else for situations or consequences that are actually their own responsibility. This is also known as "Don't look at me" syndrome. Examples: *"If you weren't so thoughtless I could be more affectionate toward you,"* or, "Something just *comes over me, and then I hit her, I can't help it, she made me do it."*

13) <u>Pedestalizing:</u> When people pedestalize, they put themselves above everyone else by operating out of a thought pattern that says they are always right? We can also pedestalize others when we over-value what they say and do. Examples: *"I told you so,"* or, *"Why can't my wife see that I'm right. She always has to contradict me."* or, *"My wife knows much better than me what's best."*

14) <u>Gold Seeking:</u> When people "gold seek," they conclude that if they do the "right" things, God will always make things go well for them in this world. They are convinced that they should be rewarded for all their good behaviors here, not just in the hereafter. Examples: *"Hard work will always win the day,"* or, *"If I keep making good meals for him, I know he'll love me."*

15) <u>Selecting:</u> When people accept only certain facts of reality, and they leave others out, this is called selecting. Examples: *"She is wonderful because she always looks so nice,"* or, *"I know that I landed the Thompson account, but that was just a fluke. Anybody could have done that. I'll never be able to get a big account like that again. I don't have what it takes."*

These 15 categories of faulty thinking are the major areas where people get into trouble. Many of us learned these types of thinking in our formative years, and have become so accustomed to them that we unconsciously adopt these thinking violations as our "standard." These thinking patterns are engrained in our mental pathways, to the point that we don't even consider their reality. Judgments like these constantly roll around in our brains like continuously playing CDs. When we encounter a situation, we often automatically start playing one of our faulty thinking CDs. These thoughts seem to have a mind of their own, acting quite independently from our own volition.

Your thinking determines the kind of world you live in. Your false self wants you to believe you have no choice. It tells you that you must follow your false self or you will ultimately perish. The result of this is that you feel separated inside, separated from your very self. You want to rid yourself of this pain, so you project it onto others. Without being consciously aware of it, you can distort your thinking and blame, criticize, judge, or otherwise attack others and your self without even recognizing the terrorist nature of your thoughts. Your true self knows that the only result of attack is more attack. All of this keeps you in turmoil because it blocks you from living in the Universal Love of God. Like a junkie hooked on drugs, your false self wants to blame and attack anyone and anything in order to stay in control, to stay alive in you.

The hope for spiritual growth dims when your mind is clogged with attack thoughts. Without the sanity of your spiritual strengths you cannot stabilize your life because you live on a roller coaster of thinking that swings you up and down, back and forth, always in contention, constant suspicion, and constant fear of attack. You must claim responsibility for what you think; otherwise the faultfinding you see in others is really only a reflection of your thinking shadow or compulsion at work with you.

The intuitive mind is a sacred gift and the rational mind is a faithful servant. We have created a society that honors the servant and has forgotten the gift.

Albert Einstein

Chapter Ten

The Five Spiritual Strengths, Shadows, and Compulsions of the Thinking Function of the Personality

Here are the five spiritual strengths of the thinking function of the personality, along with their corresponding shadows and compulsions. One of these strengths is your premier strength, the guiding strength of your thinking function. You identified your premier thinking strength when you took the *Spiritual Strengths Finder*. Of course, you're also most vulnerable to the shadow and compulsion that stand as foreboding anti-energies on either side of your premier strength.

Compulsions	Strengths	Shadows
over-zealousness <<<<<<<	**Faith**	>>>>>>>> disloyalty
perfectionism <<<<<<<<	**Wisdom**	>>>>>> inadequacy
fixatedness <<<<<<<<	**Steadfastness**	>>>> unreliability
provincialism <<<<<<<<	**Wholeness**	>>>fragmentation
servitude <<<<<<<<<	**Charity**	>>>>>>>> judgmentalism

11. Faith is …

- Being confidently loyal to God
- Having strong conviction in God's guiding hand
- Possessing fidelity, being absolutely resolute and obedient
- "Owning" a personally functional creed with universal love at the center
- Adhering in staunch and firm ways to your genuine spiritual nature

The shadow of faith is <u>disloyalty</u>

1. Resistive to established guidelines
2. Violating rules
3. Setting authority aside
4. Divided values
5. Disgracing norms and tradition
6. Disobedient to authority
7. Noncompliant and lax attitudes toward superiors
8. Unruly and undignified in presentation
9. Unscrupulous, underhanded, and sneaky in behavior
10. Rebelliousness, infidelity, betrayal

The compulsion of Faith is <u>over-zealousness</u>

1. Single minded
2. Over-identifying with a cause, project, goal, or dream
3. Thinking becomes myopic and self-absorbed
4. Unwilling, or unable, to see another's point of view
5. Mind becomes obsessed with mission

6. Carried away in efforts to bring about change
7. Discounting consequences of one's actions
8. Danger of becoming addicted to the cause
9. Blind faith in a mission, cult-like
10. Cannot be dissuaded even from wanton destruction

Hypochondriasis

Sara's Fruitless Search:

Sara is ill much of the time; sometimes she is also sick. She suffers much pain from her illnesses, and some discomfort from her sickness. Sara's several doctors know her by name and by reputation. She has had many different diagnoses; some even remain active over time.

Sara's life is punctuated by appointments ,visiting her doctors, and other medical specialists. Her week is a maze of self-imposed treatments that she gleans from all the media, searching for new ones, and round upon round of consultation with the medical community. Sara is <u>over-zealous</u> in her focus on her body, and what ails it. She 'knows' there is something wrong, and Sara's quest seems to stop at nothing trying to discover its source, finding a name for it, and rendering it solved.

Sara relegates all else in her life to a secondary position in deference to her medical issues. She is <u>disloyal</u> to her friends and family, her community and her house. Her <u>over-zealous</u> singleness of purpose and myopic vision consumes her to the point that her life is unbalanced. Sara has gradually become disloyal and neglectful of the rest of her needs outside her medical ones; she so over-emphasizes these that she eventually finds herself alienated from others, from herself, and from God. Sara's thoughts flail about in a self-absorbed conundrum of manufactured needs, finding little joy and even less peace.

While she still professes a <u>faith</u> in God, in practice even her faith life is compromised to the point where its focus is decidedly on her health, or lack of it. Sara's <u>faith</u> life has become as distorted as the rest of her life; all her prayers revolve around requests for relief from her suffering. She places her <u>faith</u> not in God's transcendent power; rather, she places her <u>faith</u> in the medical community where she continuously seeks 'salvation.' The larger questions of life meaning and existential understanding she leaves unattended. This <u>disloyalty</u> to self relegates her life to a self-centered spiral into confusion, seeking answers in places ill equipped to provide solutions.

12. Wisdom is …

- Using accumulated knowledge for the highest purposes
- Discerning spiritual qualities and the presence of love in others
- Possessing an illuminated, enlightened, and solid insight, sense, and judgment
- Being spiritually intuitive, seeing to the core motivations of another
- Recognizing the most prudent, sane, and sensible course

The shadow of wisdom is <u>inadequacy or insufficiency</u>

1. Not trusting in oneself
2. Shallow, simple, dense thinking about oneself
3. Constant thoughts of not being 'enough'
4. Clouded, folly-filled, and silly thinking
5. Persistent thoughts of personal inferiority
6. Taking no care to think accurately
7. Overlooking and even disregarding reality
8. Ill-conceived, ridiculous, indiscreet
9. Useless and even absurd self-denigration
10. Hurtful neglect of self

The compulsion of wisdom is <u>perfectionism</u>

1. Chronically dissatisfied with accomplishments
2. Needing to be 'right'
3. Excessive needs for achievement and production
4. Thinking that squeezes one's sense of accomplishment out
5. Making unrealistic demands on self and/or others
6. Insistence on ever-greater accomplishment
7. Demanding ever-increasing and 'perfect' productivity
8. Guidelines become requirements
9. Production accomplished to constantly escalating and eventually excessive standards
10. Becoming depressed when achievement is low

---<<<>>>---

Heart Disease

Richard's Perfectionism

Richard fears being 'not enough.' Since early childhood he remembers thinking that he must do his very best or risk ridicule; and ridicule is perhaps the worst suffering he could endure. To compensate for this incessant sense of <u>insufficiency</u>, Richard adopted a persona of a 'man of achievement.' He needs to produce to feel any semblance of worthiness. Watching TV or even reading for pleasure are suspect activities in his thinking because these pursuits are unproductive and therefore lacking in meaning. His sense of insecurity about his worth pushes him to produce, produce, and produce some more. If he is awake he is supposed to be engaged in achievement production. Richard can only feel worthy when he can point to a day well spent in the pursuit of achievement.

Over time, his advancing sense of personal <u>insufficiency</u> has pushed him to do more and more. And yet the feelings of <u>insufficiency</u> do not subside. He pushes harder, raises the production bar ever higher, desperately tries to evade the sense of hollowness that can envelope him if he were to relax. Vacations and weekends are consumed by fulfilling lists of tasks. He can't say 'no' to requests for fear that he would be seen as incompetent or lazy. He pursues advanced degrees, he writes books, and gives numerous presentations in the vain pursuit of a sense of personal value. He pushes his children and wife into a similar sense of accomplishment, acting as a taskmaster at times and retreating to his own personal production at other times.

One day his house of cards came tumbling down. While hurrying to finish a project so he could get to the next one, he suddenly grabbed for his chest in pain. A week later he was released from the hospital after receiving multiple coronary artery bypass surgery. It was only this that seemed to help Richard hit the reset button of his life. He was able to reconnect with the true meaning of <u>wisdom</u> and away from the perversion of <u>perfectionism</u> that had driven him for so long. With courage and hope he was able to resurrect his core wisdom power and reinvent how he lived his life.

13. Steadfastness is …

- Being fixed in place, immovable
- Being firm in belief, determined, loyal, and adherent
- Being sure of movement, unfaltering
- Having the qualities of constancy, purposefulness, dependability, and steadiness
- Being staunch, resolute, and principled

The shadow of Steadfastness is <u>unreliability</u>

1. Prone to excuses
2. Lack of self-discipline
3. Laziness
4. Disdaining of structure and protocol
5. Defensiveness
6. Irresponsibility
7. Changing reality to serve one's desires
8. Uncertain, undependable

9. Obligated to nothing, or no one but oneself
10. Unable to meet minimal requirements

The compulsion of Steadfastness is <u>fixatedness</u>

1. Pre-occupation with the past
2. Fear of the unknown
3. Dread of change
4. Blind to the reality of the need for change
5. Relationship behavior based on antiquated logic
6. Refusal to move, grow, or develop
7. Opinionated, prejudicial, arguing
8. Stubbornness
9. Compelled to keep things exactly as the are, or once were
10. Destructive resistance to constructive conversion

---<<<>>>---

Anxiety Disorder
John's Panic

fixatedness <<<<<<<<< Steadfastness >>>>> unreliability

John read the new email and began to panic. He slammed his fist on his desk and yelled, "NO!" His worst fear had now come around again; his boss was asking that he accept a transfer to a West Coast state, a move that John had declined three times before.

John was a smart, energetic, and exceptionally well-educated technology engineer. He had invested in himself early and now expected to reap the benefits of all his work. He saw his abilities as superior to his peers and exploited every opportunity to prove himself. From a distance John appeared the ideal employee, yet up close it was apparent that his steadfast demeanor and work habits covered-up a compulsion toward rigidity. John's boss was clearly aware of this and genuinely wanted to help John advance. This transfer would be a big promotion for John, but it was also a test. If John refused it a fourth time his boss had no alternative but to keep John in the same job he'd had for the past ten years.

John's thinking was stuck in a routinized, even habituated rut that prevented him from taking any risks. While his social skills were passable at work, he couldn't build deeper relationships beyond a task level, since deeper relationships required an emotional risk. John would do what he was asked, and he

would do it well, but going beyond the parameters required independent decisions that involved taking a risk. Indeed, John steadfastly avoided any geographic move, or personal growth, or change for fear of the unknown. This of course was not conscious on John's part; he actually wanted a promotion, he wanted to advance, it's just that he couldn't make the personal adjustments necessary to make this happen and sustain it.

John knew he suffered from anxiety; he was tense and rigid most of the time. Yet instead of publicly admitting his difficulty, he attempted to hide it. John describes his boyhood as a time of avoidance, a time when he was bullied by the other boys and made to feel humiliated in front of them. This "victim" mentality persists today; it's the motivation under his fear of failure, and fear of risk taking. Consequently, John protects himself in all ways possible, from large insurance policies to the type of automobile he drives. John can be defensive, even stubborn. He'll rationalize his rigid thinking by arguing the logic of his position, something he's quite skilled at. John would like a long-term relationship but so far his attempts have proved inadequate, and so John lives a life without a partner.

As conscientious as John may be at work he suffers from the shadow of <u>unreliability</u> regarding himself. His home remains undecorated, even after years of living there, house maintenance is postponed, he rarely cleans, and there are no pictures on the walls. John's home reflects the starkness of his interior life. The exterior of his house appears presentable, as does John's personal exterior, however its interior, like his own interior, remains disheveled.

John gradually came to realize his predicament. He slowly moved toward a new life fullness by focusing on his primary spiritual strength of <u>steadfastness</u>. He became more sensitive to his true inner needs and less sensitive to how he was being perceived. He let-go of his need for sameness and began to inject small changes into his world. Most of all John gave himself permission to take a risk.

14. Wholeness is ...

- The state of being intact, complete, undivided ... having integrity
- Being entirely undiminished ... an unbroken unit
- Possessing the quality of concentration toward one goal
- Unity with universal love
- Achieving togetherness with universal love and love's ways
- Attaining personality coherence
- The state of personal unity
- Being undivided, full, and powerful
- Interest in many, even conflicting spiritual paths
- Searching for the global, overarching, truths

The shadow of wholeness is <u>fragmentation</u>

1. Threatened by conflict, withdraw from complex situations
2. Scattered, irrelevant thinking
3. Alienated, broken, fearful, and anxious
4. Frustrated, disconnected, dashed
5. Having no purpose, off-balance, in vain
6. Dreary, sulking, collapsed
7. Powerless, unsupported, discouraged
8. Broken, disconnected, and off-balance thinking
9. Broken, rendered weak, impotent
10. Collapsed and unrepairable

The compulsion of wholeness is <u>provincialism</u>

1. Narrow and constricted thinking
2. Shallow, uninteresting and dull thinking
3. Prone to gossip, nit picking, feeling superior
4. Limited and parochial thinking
5. Having no global thinking
6. Uni-dimensional, singular, petty, and confined thinking
7. Restriction of thought to small area or scope
8. Thinking becomes limited and anemic
9. Over-focusing on details and missing the whole
10. No new ideas

---<<<>>>---

Multiple Sclerosis (MS)
Amy's Wholeness

Amy rested her head back down on her pillow after just giving herself her weekly injection in her thigh, a medicine to control the symptoms and slow down the progression of her MS. She felt exhausted. But more than physically fatigued, she was overwhelmed by a rush of emotion that further robbed her of the little energy and hope that she tried so valiantly to hold onto. Amy's world had become very small, and her thinking quite provincial.

It's been 10 years since her diagnosis of MS, and all things considered, she's doing fairly well. She can work, although not full time as she would like, and she maintains friendships and family ties which are lifelines for her now since her husband left her three years ago. After the divorce she felt like her life was in pieces on the floor in front of her. All her thoughts ran to the fact of her fragmentation, weakness, and simply being personally unbalanced. She thought of herself as disconnected from life, alienated, broken, and scattered. Her world had collapsed, she thought, and she was often despairing that it would ever come back together. Her thoughts became narrow and provincial; they swirled around and around in a senseless random spiral leading her nowhere. That was until she met Stan at her local hospital MS support group.

Stan was at first frightening to her because his MS had put him in a wheelchair, something Amy tried and hoped with everything in her to avoid. Yet there was something about this man that intrigued her, it wasn't a romantic attraction, rather it was a spiritual one. Stan was an inspiration, he had such personal integrity; he seemed so comfortable in his skin. He possessed the quality of personality coherence; everything seemed to 'fit together' in and with Stan. Amy felt herself more at peace and <u>whole</u> when she was around him; he was so powerful in his own way, so sure of himself without being the slightest bit arrogant or boastful. Stan was real, genuine, and simply 'together.' Stan was <u>whole</u>!

As Amy gradually realized the <u>wholeness</u> in Stan she began rethinking her life situation, and rose to a new spiritual level. She gained new strength, new purpose in life, and an internal sensation that all would be well even if her MS worsened. Amy began to pick up the pieces of her life, her ailing body, her broken marriage, and her dashed dreams. She thought new thoughts about all of this, and more. Her relationship with her two sons improved markedly, her job became more interesting and satisfying, her friends seemed more present to her, and she was noticeably happier. Amy had moved out of the illness of depression that attended her MS, and rose to know that she was OK, that everything would be alright, and that she was now whole too. Here was Amy's healing.

15. Charity is …

- Having unconditional benevolent goodwill
- Giving and expecting nothing in return
- Helping other people in a selfless manner
- Recognizing the needs of another and giving in a big-hearted manner
- Possessing and using forgiveness and altruism
- Selfless, big-hearted, forgiving, resilient

- Energetic offering of self
- Honoring another without dishonoring oneself

The shadow of charity is <u>judgmentalism</u>

1. Repeatedly projecting your opinion upon another
2. Affronting and maligning toward another
3. Malevolence, ruthless, ill-natured
4. Cynical and negative thinking
5. Condemnation and attacking thoughts
6. Chronic criticism of self and/or others
7. Acrimonious, non-compassionate, ferocity
8. Spiteful, surly, virulent, vindictive
9. Rancor and vindictiveness.
10. Revengeful … holding grudges

The compulsion of charity is <u>servitude</u>

1. Cognitive/mental submission
2. Placing oneself in submissive service to another
3. Involuntarily subjecting one's thoughts to a "master"
4. Relinquishing personal ownership of thoughts
5. Blind service
6. Self-deprecating thinking
7. Giving up freedom of thought
8. Loss of the liberty
9. Slavish devotion to another's wishes
10. Loss of self-determination

Critical Personality
Frank's Charity

Frank is a giver; he is the proverbial "give you the shirt off my back" kind of guy. Frank helps everyone he can, and because he is so handy and seems to know so much about so much, Frank finds himself in constant demand. His friends, family, neighbors, church members, etc. clamor for more of Frank. And Frank seems so ever ready to respond. Truly, Frank is a paragon of <u>charity</u>.

But he struggles with his dark shadow of <u>judging</u>; Frank can be blaming, picking, and down right critical. This is not the persona Frank shows to the world, but Frank's wife knows about his criticism; she regularly endures Frank's sharp barbs and condemning tone of voice. Frank can't let things go; he confronts and affronts her at every turn. Soon she becomes frustrated and even vindictive, she finds herself becoming very passive around him, especially after his negative attacks. Frank not only attacks her, he routinely criticizes some of the very people he helps. *"They don't know what they're doing."* Or *"They couldn't find their way out of a paper bag."* are common remarks from Frank.

Yet Frank carries on with this double life of being pleasant, helpful, and accommodating on the outside, while being critical, blaming, condemning, and ridiculing on the inside. Frank knows he's a giver, but at the same time he sees the rest of the world as takers, and without being consciously aware of his internal contradiction, he resents it. So Frank carries on in an almost self-deprecating manner of submission and <u>servitude</u>. He appears blind to his internal paradox; it's almost as though

Frank is a slave to his own lack of self-examination, he trips over his thinking that in order to be charitable he must always subdue any thoughts of self fulfillment. Frank defers all of his own needs onto others, and, consequently, feels put upon, taken advantage of, and taken for granted. In reality, of course, none of this thinking is true, it's all figments of Frank's internal tension between his spiritual strength of <u>charity</u>, and its shadow of <u>judgment</u> and compulsion of <u>servitude</u>.

Frank needs to find the core of his spiritual strength of charity. <u>Charity</u> is unselfish, yet, as the old adage goes, 'charity begins at home.' Frank doesn't give to himself and his family; he dishonors the very people he loves. The second part of the great Christian commandment, that is echoed in every other faith tradition as well, is that '*we must love our neighbors as ourselves.*" We must first love ourselves before we can truly love (be charitable) others. Frank doesn't love himself; he carries on an internal dialogue of thinking that deprecates himself as somehow unworthy. Here is where Frank needs healing.

Chapter Eleven
Personality Function Four: Feeling

How your personality creates your emotional life

Your feelings are the emotional facts of your 'now.' Asked how you're feeling, and you immediately try to come up with a word or words that fit your internal emotional sensations. This is harder to do than you might think. Psychiatry uses a term for the inability to connect feelings sensations with words; the term is *alexithymia*. Alexithymia literally means having no words for feelings. We're all a bit alexithymic, we can all remember a time when we became verbally paralyzed when asked how we felt about something. Some of us however are so alexithymic that we can hardly find any word at all, at any time, to describe how we're feeling emotionally; it's as though there is an emotional disconnect between our feelings and our thinking.

Words that help us understand the depth and breadth of feelings include: heartache, transformation, impressions, enter into the spirit of the moment, sentiment, emotions, affected by, moved by, inspired by, troubled by, heart & soul, devout, being touched, being moved, emote, pull your heart strings, having a 'spell,' in reverie, euphoric (emotionally up) or dysthymic (emotionally down), histrionic, and being wooden, to name a few.

147

Feelings are the automatic consequences of your thoughts; every thought, or thought bundle immediately generates a feeling or bundle of feelings. Interestingly, you have the least volitional influence over your personality feeling function than you do of any of the other five functions. However, you do have immense influence over to what degree and how long a feeling takes up residence in you.

So much of your overall emotional health is determined by your feelings, because your feelings determine your mood more than any other personality force. When you feel 'good' you're generally in a positive mood, and of course you know that the opposite is true as well. You've had down days, sad times, a sour disposition, and a dour temperament at times. Depression, chronic or cyclical feelings of sadness, anger, irritability or just plain melancholia, seems part of the fabric of our times.

Dr. Gerald Jampolsky claims that all feelings come from only two basic feelings states: love and fear. If you could count all the feelings words in the dictionary and place them in these two categories, you'd find that the 'fear' list would be twice as long as the 'love' list. Perhaps we're all still suffering from the fear we felt as primitives in the forest? Anthony Robbins echoes Dr. Jampolsky's thinking on this point; Robbins also divides all feelings into two categories: 1) enabling feelings, like joy, confidence, energized, and the like, and 2) paralyzing feelings, like confusion, disillusionment, shame, guilt and the like.

Sigmund Freud had an interesting 'take' on feelings. He started from the premise that we all feel like orphans here on earth:

abandoned, alone, separated, and disconnected. Freud said that our basic emotional identity as orphans compels us to want to go home. He theorized that your mother's womb was this home. He concluded that since the inutuero time was the only time of your existence when you felt no need, it's there where you'd like to return. Consequently Freud developed a psychology based on psychosexual developmental steps: oral, anal, genital stages, etc. Actually, many people think that Freud had a great idea there, but unfortunately he had the wrong place. They would point out that since we come from God, or Universal Love, that this is the existential 'place' where we want to return. Some would say that your true-self inner voice speaks softly to you beckoning you to return home, the place of your true reality.

The Depressions

Depression has been termed the emotional 'common cold' of our times. Certainly the diagnosis of depression is made more often, and antidepressant medications are now second only to cholesterol medications in total prescriptions written. Yet, even though we think of depression as a singular emotional disorder, it's actually as unique as the personality that experiences it. The genders experience depression differently, women usually exhibit more sadness, fatigue, and sensitivity, while men seem to exhibit more anger, irritability, and impulsiveness when depressed. Such generalizations may help us be more vigilant to the prevalence of depression, but they are quite academic for us individually. The best I can say about it is that there is not one depression, but many depressions. Just like there are many cancers, depression comes in almost as many presentations as there are people suffering from depression.

Common Symptoms of Major Depression

1. Persistent sad, anxious, or "empty" mood.
2. Feelings of hopelessness or pessimism.
3. Feelings of guilt, worthlessness, helplessness.
4. Loss of interest or pleasure in hobbies and activities that were once enjoyed.
5. Insomnia, early morning awakening, or excessive sleeping.
6. Appetite and weight loss or overeating and weight gain.
7. Decreased energy, fatigue, feeling "slowed down."
8. Thoughts of death or suicide.
9. Restlessness and irritability.
10. Difficulty concentrating, remembering, making decisions.
11. Persistent physical symptoms that do not respond to treatment, such as headaches, digestive disorders, and chronic pain.

Note: One needn't have all these symptoms to be diagnosed as depressed. Intensity and duration of symptoms determines the depth of the depression.

Dealing with your feelings

Some common negative ways of dealing with feelings include:

1. **Stuff your feelings.** This psychological maneuver is also known as hiding or burying your feelings. Think of a

sack inside you that looks like a pillowcase with a drawstring tie. Each time you experience a feeling you don't want, you simply stuff it into your internal sack. At first it's rather easy; there's plenty of room. After a time, however, the sack starts filling up. It gets bigger and bigger. Finally, you have stuffed so much into your sack that it begins to weaken along the seams. The acid of your negative, unclarified feelings begins to leak out. Into what does this toxic acid leak? It leaks into your bowels, and your heart, and your gallbladder, and your mood, and all kinds of places. It also leaks into your shadows and compulsions where it produces illness.

The unfortunate thing about stuffing your feelings is that most people are unaware that they're even doing it. It happens automatically. You stuff your feelings because you're afraid of something. You fear some unknown power. Eventually, after you have stuffed so many of your feelings, never letting them see the light of day, you may begin to suffer from what Alcoholics Anonymous calls "frozen feelings." You become numb to your feelings altogether.

If thoughts <u>seek</u> expression, feelings <u>find</u> expression, and if you aren't aware of what you're feeling, you can place yourself at risk for your feelings to take hold of you rather than the other way around. Your feelings start expressing themselves in ways and in places that push you out to your shadows and your compulsions. When this begins, it's hard to gain some genuine understanding of your feelings; a deep enough understanding so you can let them do their job, which is to activate your spiritual strengths.

2. **Resist, fight, or otherwise deny your feelings.** The second unhealthy way you can deal with your feelings is similar to the first. However, when you resist, fight, and deny your feelings, you are more aware of what you're doing. Still, your feelings remain so vague or shrouded that you don't deal with them honestly. Instead, you resist and fight your feelings. In effect, you tell them, *"You shouldn't be here!"* You expend colossal amounts of energy in doing this and, of course, it does nothing but deplete you. Paradoxically, your efforts to banish your feelings will actually accomplish the exact opposite. Battling feelings keeps the emotions close at hand, right up in the forefront of your perception and thinking. If the feeling tries to run away from your internal wrath, you manage to yank it back to continue the fight once again.

3. **Project your feelings.** Another way of not dealing with your feelings is to dump or project them onto other people or things. This piece of psychological engineering works something like this: when the tired and haggard man comes home from work feeling defeated and rejected, his first reaction is to kick the dog, as if his terrible day is somehow the dog's fault. Projecting is something like this, taking our feeling out on others, blaming them for our unfortunate emotional fix.

When you dump your feelings in this way, you do it quite unconsciously. The procedure becomes automatic and eventually habitual. You develop favorite or standard ways of dealing with your feelings and seem to use them over and over again like those comfortable old loafers that are waiting for you every Saturday morning. Unfortunately these old loafers, these habitual ways of dealing with your feelings are harmful, not helpful, for you. They may be initially comfortable, but in the long run they pinch and confine your feet until you've can't wait to take them off.

4. **Disguise your feelings.** The final negative way you can deal with your unwanted feelings is to make them something other than what they are. This is also known as the *Houdini* trick. You can convert your worst feelings into something more comfortable without the slightest bit of internal awareness that you are indeed doing this. Examples of this are using reckless humor to cover up embarrassment or expressing anger when you actually feel sad or hurt.

   The degree to which you are aware of your feelings, and aware that you are consciously making a decision regarding them, is the same degree to which you are reaching for high-level psychological and spiritual wellness … and in the process finding healing. Awareness of your feelings spells the difference between thriving in life and sleepwalking through it, between health and illness.

Healthy Ways of Dealing With Your Feelings

1. **Express your feelings.** Expressing your feelings does not mean you slather your emotions all over every person you meet. Rather it means giving yourself permission to express your feelings in a place and in a way of your choice. You are never obliged to express all your feelings, nor could you, since your feelings are many times contradictory – one way on this day, and another way on that day. Expressing your feelings means taking active, deliberate steps to communicate the major emotional themes that emerge in you.

2. **Consciously decide to do nothing at all with your feelings.** There is no law that says you are compelled to express all your feelings. An elementary school principal was in her office having a curriculum meeting with another teacher when a third teacher poked her head in the door asking what to do about a particular boy who was making grotesque noises and disrupting her class. When the principal gave the teacher her answer that she would do nothing right now, the teacher retorted, *"Sometimes I think your heart is made of marshmallow."* The principal felt startled and didn't have time to react. She later found herself perplexed, embarrassed, and slightly angry that this teacher would criticize her in front of another teacher. Later she reviewed the incident in her mind and decided with clarified awareness that she would take no action at all. She examined the thoughts that gave her negative feelings. She modified them by realizing that the

teacher in question was having some physical problems lately. She reasoned that these problems might have played a role in somewhat inappropriate comment. The principal made a conscious decision to simply accept her feelings as they were and not express them directly. This is healthy.

3. **Allow your feelings to wash over you.** Imagine any feelings you have as an approaching wave at the beach. You can see it coming, but your first reaction is fear. Allowing the feeling to wash over you means to actually feel the depth of the feeling as it strikes. Try to sense the feeling totally. Try to 'see' it, 'touch' it, 'smell' it, 'hear' it, and 'taste' it. Try to be with the feeling, letting it crash around you.

4. **Diffuse your feelings by changing the thoughts that generated them in the first place.** This method was discussed in chapter eight. Remember the 15 negative judgments? Modifying your thoughts is a sure way to diffuse the sting of feelings that flow from such judgments. Your goal is thought accuracy. You want your thinking to accurately describe reality, not some illusionary nightmare thinking that distorts reality and generates feelings of fear.

BIDFARE

You can do little to prevent feelings from rushing in, but you can do quite a bit to influence them once they arrive. I've devised a little mnemonic devise to help you process your feelings. I call it the BIDFARE method. Here's how it works:

B – Become aware that your are experiencing feeling(s)
I – Identify the feeling(s)
D – Decide what you want to do with this feeling(s)
F – Figure where the thought(s) that generated this feeling(s) originated
A – Affirm yourself with a new thought(s)
R – Reassess the feeling(s)
E – Elope to peace

Let's unpack this process.

Become Aware – Becoming aware of your feelings is sometimes not easy. I see patients regularly who are alexithymic and genuinely aren't aware that they are experiencing feelings. Anger is a particularly difficult feeling for some people. Perhaps because we've been taught not to show anger, we lapse into an emotional numbness where our affect is unavailable to us. I work very hard as a counselor helping people 'get in touch with their feelings.' This is a competency that can be learned, or at least thawed out; either way, becoming aware of your emotional internal terrain is a mandatory step toward optimal living and mental health.

Identify Your Feelings -- Once you know that you're experiencing feelings, you need to put a name on it or them. Naming your feelings is not easy either. Most of us come from families where feelings were regarded as suspect, and consequently we weren't taught a very robust feelings vocabulary. We need to teach ourselves. It helps to have a list of feelings you can use as reference. I have a "Feelings Wheel" on my counseling office wall that's very helpful. I regularly have patients consult it to figure out the best words to describe their current feelings. Just naming your feelings provides certain emancipation from the tyranny of chronic feelings, and gives you a sense of mastery over them.

Decide – You generally have two options for your feelings; you either want to 1) extend 'love' feelings, or 2) extinguish 'fear' feelings. Either way, you need to discern where this feeling comes from: your feelings function 1) spiritual strength, 2) your shadow, or 3) your compulsion. If the feeling comes from your strength, chances are you want to extend it; conversely if it/they come from either your shadow or compulsion you generally want to extinguish it. Again, just making this conscious decision is very helpful; it allows you to inch closer to gaining mastery over your feelings, rather than the other way around. If the feeling comes from your shadow or compulsion, ask yourself, "what would my spiritual strength convert this feeling into a more constructive feeling?

Figure Out – Your thoughts generate your feelings. If you can gain an understanding of which thought or thoughts might have generated this feelings state, you can not only try to avoid such inaccurate, shadow thinking in the future, you can also begin the process of replacing these noxious thoughts with ones that emerge from your thinking function spiritual strength.

Affirm Yourself – No one is forcing you to think or to feel in any particular way; you're free to think the way you believe is best for you, and you're free to change your mind anytime.

Experiment by 'trying on' lots of different thoughts and see how they feel; it can be fun and certainly freeing.

Reassess – Once you've determined a new thought and put it into your personality, now it's time to reassess your feelings. Generally you can't completely obliterate paralyzing feeling right away, but you can certainly take the sting out of them. Let's say your original thought was generating a noxious feeling at the 80% level; wouldn't it be a personal success if your new thought could lower that feeling to the 25% level? Certainly you'd feel better afterward and you'd be transferring the energy that you formerly used to support the feeling at the 80% down to the 25% level, energy that you can put to better use somewhere else in your personality.

Elope – Elope to peace! If you can do this with all your noxious feelings, imagine the new peace that can accrue to you in the process. Feeling pressured and even 'burned-out' really means that you've been wasting your energy (you only have 100% you know) supporting feelings and thoughts from your shadows and compulsions.

Purposes of Anger, the secondary emotion

Anger may be the most ubiquitous paralyzing feeling we can experience. Anger can be destructive to others as much as it is to us. Yet, anger is generally the result of an amalgam of other feelings that we fail to deal with as they arise within us. These primary feelings build until they congeal into what we call anger.

It's said that anger is a mature human emotion as long as it fulfills two criteria: 1) it doesn't hurt anyone, and, 2) it doesn't last more than five minutes. This five-minute time limit is a bit "tongue-in-cheek" yet it does give a time boundary on anger. When anger persists it "morphs" into holding a grudge; a most noxious and personality damaging condition. Anger is so prevalent because it works! And just what does anger do? The answer becomes clear when you look at the purposes of anger.

1. To protect from closeness with others
2. To avoid possible rejection
3. To alter the behavior of others
4. To protect against the recurrence of disliked behavior
5. To disguise feelings of hurt
6. To disguise alienation
7. To demand your 'rights'
8. To manifest your 'shoulds'
9. To dump' long held baggage
10. As an expression of genuine indignation

Feelings are good windows for getting a quick glance into the operations of your personality. As you become more, 1) aware of your feelings, 2) facile in identifying them, and 3) increasingly adept at methods for extending enabling feelings, and 4) disposing of paralyzing feelings, you'll notice a new sense of personal empowerment emerge in you ... this too is part of your healing journey.

Chapter Twelve

The Five Spiritual Strengths, Shadows, and Compulsions of the Feeling Function of the Personality

Here are the five spiritual strengths of the feeling function of the personality, along with their corresponding shadows and compulsions. One of these strengths is your premier strength, the guiding strength of your feeling function. You identified your premier feeling strength when you took the *Spiritual Strengths Finder*. Of course, you're also most vulnerable to the shadow and compulsion that stand as foreboding anti-energies on either side of your premier strength.

Compulsions	Strengths	Shadows
hyperphoria <<<<<<< **Joy** >>>>>>>> dejection		
reductionism <<<<<< **Trust** >>>>>>> insecurity		
pollyannaism <<<<<< **Love-Finder** >> fault-seeker		
ingratiating <<<<<<< **Empathy** >>>>> obtuseness		
submissiveness <<<< **Gratitude** >>>>> blaming		

16. Joy is …

- Expressing pleasure or delight in celebration
- Showing great happiness of heart
- The unspoken, inner result of knowing that universal love is your true reality
- Your positive emotional response to knowing that universal love grace sustains you
- Being jubilant or inwardly elated knowing you will be offered God's grace throughout your life
- Free spirited, elated exuberance, jubilant.
- Knowing one's connection to God.
- Being 'wonder-filled'

The shadow of Joy is dejection

1. Saddened of heart and spirit
2. Emotionally flat
3. Dispirited, cheerless, dreary
4. In the doldrums
5. Uncomfortable and alone
6. Downcast, brooding, sulky
7. Gloomy, melancholic, dismal
8. To lose heart
9. Depression, weighted, oppressed
10. Lost, despairful, hopeless

The compulsion of Joy is hyperphoria

1. Abnormal feelings of buoyant vigor and health
2. Emotionally "high" beyond appropriate limits

3. Excessive feelings of positive mood
4. Experiencing frequent rushes of energy
5. Devil-may-care attitude, caution to the wind
6. Setting aside normal proprietary boundaries of affect
7. Flight from any pain and/or discomfort
8. Persistent euphoria, perhaps masking depressed affect
9. Having no limits
10. Becoming frenetic to the point of desperation

Breast Cancer
Kristen's Bombshell

At 27 years old and feeling just great Kristen knew this second pregnancy was much different. Kristen's first pregnancy made her sick for nine months, but this second one was a dream. At the seven-month mark she felt a small lump in her right breast, but quickly dismissed it as a clogged milk duct; *"I didn't even tell my doctor about it."* At her first post-delivery appointment with her doctor two weeks after a marvelously smooth birth and perfect baby girl, Kristen did ask about the lump that still remained. Her doctor minimized it, but did send her for an ultrasound, which showed a mass.

Kristen's emotions sank from jubilation to utter <u>dejection</u>. Her thoughts moved to the worst outcomes. *"This is cancer, I just knew it in my heart,"* she thought.   One set of negative thoughts ignited another, and another. Soon Kristen was beyond <u>dejection</u> – she was depressed. The day came for her consultation with a surgeon who in a two-hour marathon enumerated all that could go wrong, this pushed Kristen into desperation, her darkest hour after the trauma of diagnosis. Kristen consulted a spiritual coach and found that she herself had successfully dealt with breast cancer some years earlier.

Kristen decided she needed a new surgeon and found one who related well and easily with her. The six months of chemotherapy started almost immediately. Right from the *get go* she felt the nausea, fatigue, the low blood counts, and she, of course, lost her hair. Kristen was emotionally down in the dumps. Two weeks later they inserted a clavicle port for easier chemotherapy. But the port was more than difficult. In lots of physical pain from the port, and even more emotional pain, Kristen descended even deeper into a <u>dejected</u> depression. In her despair, she prayed harder than she ever had. *"Dear Lord, I can't do this on my own. I'm giving all this to you. You must carry me through,"* she prayed.

Upon awakening the next day Kristen was saturated in peace and a resolute sense of pure <u>joy</u>. *"I had no more port pain, no more nausea, and my energy was back up. I felt a new calmness that I had never experienced before."* Even though she knew she wasn't abandoned, Kristen asked for signs – and they were given! She saw rainbows several days in succession; she felt a new appreciation for her husband, her perfect children, and her supportive parents. The <u>joy</u> of living swept over her. She realized that the hair she lost wasn't her, that her real being was the intangible peace and <u>joy</u> of knowing, not simply believing, but knowing that God was with her and she would be OK. *"I placed myself in God's hands and I felt a new sense of* connectedness with everything and everyone. *My fears were gone – replaced by joy."* And the joy just kept coming, even though the chemotherapy continued as well. *"I was pregnant for a reason. My only question now is, 'How can I use my experience to help others?'"*

And the signs of divine presence kept coming too. A family friend gave her a bottle of Lourdes holy water. Each night before her bath, Kristen blesses herself with the water and sprinkles a few drops on her breasts. *"I've been doing this every day for months now, and the water level in the bottle hasn't gone down."* Kristen has no doubt that this is also divine work.

Kristen remains joyful even though she faces a double mastectomy soon. The dark clouds of dejection have cleared fully to reveal her true spiritual strength of joy – a gift of love and life that Kristen now sees as her true self. *"All my personal second guessing is gone. Today I'm fine, I'm whole, and I'm joyous."*

17. Trust is …

- Assured reliance on God
- A mature dependence on universal love
- Believing in and expecting with confidence that love's promise of abundance is being fulfilled, even now
- Anticipating that all things and events will eventually turn out good
- Consigning your life to love's care

The shadow of Trust is <u>insecurity</u>

1. Not firmly fastened or fixed
2. Emotionally shaky
3. Feeling uncertain and/or unsafe
4. Not highly stable
5. Lacking inner confidence
6. Feeling vulnerable, not adequately protected
7. Deficient in assurance
8. Beset by anxiety
9. Excessive avoiding-type behaviors
10. Fear of failure, shame, ridicule, and potential rejection

The compulsion of Trust is <u>reductionism</u>

1. Accepting simple formulas and elementary solutions to life
2. Makes rules from guidelines
3. Hiding behind rules and laws
4. Needing pat, black-and-white answers
5. Dependence on outside pronouncements
6. Narrowness of perspective...abhorrence of change
7. Personal security derived from singular source
8. Worship of what was, nostalgic
9. Excessive attachment to a highly directive force
10. Controlled by association to an "authority"

---<<<>>>---

Obsessive Compulsive Disorder
Stacey's Fretfulness

Stacey couldn't seem to get out the door to her hair appointment. She paced back and forth between the stove and the toaster. She stared at the knobs on the stove, *"Were they truly in the 'off' position?* she questioned. She went to the toaster and asked herself the same question only to have this thought eclipsed by another, *"What about the gas water heater?" "Did I smell gas in the basement the other day?"* She checked and rechecked all the appliances as well as all the windows and doors to make sure they were locked, before she finally could go to her garage. She held her skirt tightly to her legs as she walked through the garage for fear that she might brush against something, anything, and become somehow contaminated.

Stacey is continuously uncertain about, well, just about everything. As a single woman, she is especially <u>insecure</u> about maintenance issues around her house. Indecision is her chronic companion, yet she seeks advice from only a very few people, fearing that others might think less of her. Her psychological guard is always 'up.' While she suffers a severe sense of personal <u>insecurity</u>, she seeks only the most concrete and sure answers to her continuous torrent of questions. Stacey only infrequently ventures beyond her house; driving her car raises abundant fears, especially the fear that she might somehow hurt someone.

Perhaps because of her interior anxieties, Stacey seeks solidity outside of herself. Unable to trust her own personal principles for living, she struggles to <u>reduce</u> life to simple, black-and-white regulations from outside of her, especially from her church. She wants someone or something else to tell her what to think, and what actions are 'right' and best, in a purely <u>reductionistic</u> manner. Lacking internal structures that give her peace, she is dependent upon others to 'show her the way.' Stacey wants to <u>reduce</u> life to a short list of do's and don'ts, to a simple formula that she can use to organize and operate her life. She seeks asylum from the inherent mystery of life by imposing rules, laws, and regulations upon it, thereby removing indecision and instead relying on sameness. Stacey always wants today to be just like yesterday.

Stacey desperately needs her spiritual strength of <u>trust</u>. She needs to <u>trust</u> the very power she already possesses within. The idea of trusting her feelings, or even depending on her conscience for guidance, is outside her realm of possibility. Her conception of God is that of a stern judge who is demanding and critical, consequently she feels confused, rattled, beset by insecurity, and fearful of wrongdoing. Stacey is a bright person, but her intelligence is eclipsed by her feelings of insecurity, confusion, and anxiety. The power of <u>trust</u>, the energy of love is her only answer, so she can live the mystery of life rather than trying to discover a solution to life.

18. Love-Finder is ...

- Feeling God's hand in everything
- Awakening to love everywhere
- Continuously discovering the presence of God
- Constantly detecting love in your self
- Always recognizing the healing/transforming power of love within
- Surrender to God

- Seeing God's presence in all things.
- Experiencing the eternal silence.

The shadow of Love-Finder is <u>faultfinder</u>

1. Finding blemishes, defects, or imperfections to an excessive degree
2. Seeing only 'one way'
3. Imposing excessive responsibility or accountability on self and/or others
4. Prone to see failing, frailty, or foible
5. Overly critical and negativistic
6. Uses humor recklessly, such as sarcasm
7. Self-Deceptive, false expectations
8. Self critical, petty, pessimistic
9. Dejected, censuring of self and others
10. Chronically angry

The compulsion of Love-Finder is <u>pollyannaism</u>

1. Seeing the world through "rose colored glasses"
2. Self-permission to feel only positive or fanciful feelings
3. Compelled to feel only positivism, goodwill, and peace
4. Disregards full range of human feelings
5. Excludes shadows and compulsions from emotions
6. Feelings elude reality...overly optimistic to a fault
7. Rejects all emotions except goodwill and peace, harmony and grace
8. Exaggerated compliments, blind positive regard
9. Total and complete happiness become one's only realities
10. Lives in "la-la" land

Living in Fantasy
Mario's Unreality

Mario dialed his cell phone calling the fourth person today while on his daily walk. Mario likes talking; actually he craves telling others some of his ideas about life, his interpretations of the world condition, right off the top of his head. As a clear extravert Mario seeks conversations because he does his clearest thinking, and therefore experiences his most satisfying feelings, when talking to others … even strangers!

In his heart Mario is a loving and compassionate person, however in this third year as a stockbroker some small but troublesome changes have appeared. Formerly balanced and even-handed in his feelings toward self and others, Mario has 'morphed' into what could only be termed an affect of pollyannaism. He never tires of exposing the most encouraging and positive aspects of any life situation or person. On and on he can spin his perspective of energizing feelings. His view of life is decidedly rose colored; he never sees, or allows himself to experience feelings other than goodwill and peace, harmony and grace. Mario is never confrontive, rather he is ever careful to overindulge his topic with an exaggerated spin of compliments that bespeak only excessive positive regard. His compulsion pulls him to fanatical optimism that he could not contain. Mario is visibly uncomfortable when others do not agree, tacitly or otherwise, with what he is 'selling' today.

Negativism is outside of Mario's realm. Indeed he sees no faults nor any transgression or idiosyncrasies of even a minor key in anyone or anything. Mario simply doesn't let feelings other than positive ones into his psyche. Mario seems incapable of offering any <u>faultfinding</u>, however constructive it may be; his <u>pollyannaism</u> borders on self-deception. He lives in an inaccurate confluence of feelings that skew his emotions into his unique unreality. His overemphasis of perceptions and thinking in the direction of exaggerated positivism blinds him even to his true reality. Unable or unwilling to affectively register any feelings less than exuberant give Mario something of an ingenuine feel. Paradoxically this very trait moves others to initially frame Mario in a most attractive light. Yet, his insistence on hyperbole, not only distorts his own reality, but also eventually forces others to subtly doubt or even discount some of Mario's ideas. While he is marvelously entertaining at times, his rosy appraisals and affective inflations cause others to internally question his conclusions, which tends to undermine whatever confidence they might ordinarily have in Mario's words.

Mario needs to discover his center of <u>love-finding</u>. <u>Love-finding</u> means seeking the effects of loving action, but it does not mean smearing everything with a false whitewash of sentimental love. Love is everywhere, to be sure, but so are the shadows and compulsions of love. Our goal is to be accurate in all the functions of our personality – not overly selective in one direction or the other.

19. Empathy is ...

- Being totally 'with' the children of love (everyone)
- Understanding abundantly the total experiences of another
- Becoming acutely aware of the totality of another's feelings as a profound expression of emotional intimacy

- Walking in another's emotional 'shoes'
- Wanting to 'be with' another.
- Compelled to 'save' another from pain.

The shadow of Empathy is <u>obtuseness.</u>

1. Inert, impassive, dull.
2. Blunt, callous, cold.
3. Unconcerned, indifferent, numb.
4. Unfeeling, insensible, unmoved.
5. Untouched, apathetic, taking no interest.
6. Unable to discern emotional needs of self and others.
7. Avoidant of emotions
8. No emotional intelligence
9. Emotionally rigid
10. Alexathymic

The compulsion of Empathy is <u>ingratiating.</u>

1. Contorting oneself to gain another's favor or good graces
2. Over-complimenting others so as to manipulate their feelings
3. Sense that others <u>must</u> like you
4. Work tirelessly in service of praise or merit from others
5. Excessive attempts at currying favor
6. Depending on others for one's self-worth
7. Sacrificing one's values to gain approval
8. Giving-up of self to curry favor
9. Live a *Janus*-like, two-faced life
10. Losing touch with one's unique reality

---<<<>>>---

Battered Marriage
Brandy's Discontent

Brandy dropped her three children off at school and was off to work. On the way she caught herself thinking of her husband now living apart from her. His uncertainty about their relationship had driven him to live independently; it had the opposite effect upon Brandy.

Brandy is a 'feeling person,' able to accurately pinpoint other's feelings quite keenly. Brandy never tires of searching for the motivation behind the actions of others. Her intuition is clean, sharp, and incisive; her ability to discern feelings in others is nothing short of extraordinary. She 'sees' into others through a very clear lens, so much so that Brandy is able to calculate others' next behaviors with uncanny accuracy. Brandy is a formidable emotional presence wherever she goes and with whomever she interacts.

Yet, Brandy is decidedly obtuse to her own needs. She focuses almost entirely on her husband's needs and wants, and those of her three children. She is perhaps the only person she has ever 'met' about whom she is emotionally insensitive. It seems that Brandy has emotional insight into everyone else but herself. This blind spot pushes her to focus almost entirely upon her children and her husband. Her emotional alienation from herself makes her rather immature about her interior life. She can't delve into her own feelings, or understand her own motivations. This affective ineptitude robs her of a necessary ingredient in her marriage ...true intimate communication with

173

her husband. He was raised in a rather distant cold and insensitive family, which now makes him long for deeper intimate connections. Their mutual unmet needs, her need for a deeper self-knowledge, and his need for deeper emotional connection, pushes their marriage to the tipping point of separation.

True empathy allows a person to emotionally 'know' others and oneself. Brandy needs to unblock her empathy; it appears over-developed when applied to others, but clearly under-developed regarding herself. Brandy's current use of her spiritual strength of empathy causes a hyper-focus on her husband and a corresponding hypo-focus on her own emotional needs and desires. At one and the same time, Brandy is both obtuse and ingratiating; she's obtuse to herself and ingratiating to her husband. This emotional imbalance damages her ability to relate to the very people she loves the most, her husband, who she genuinely loves with everything in her, and her children.

20. Gratitude is …

- Expressing profound thankfulness
- Adopting a worshipful attitude toward your God for giving so abundantly; for giving you unmerited divine assistance throughout your life
- Giving continuous praise to God
- Adoration coupled with a sense of sanctification
- Recognizing the giftedness in which you live
- Sensing the amazing abundance
- Appreciation of others

The shadow of Gratitude is <u>blaming</u>.

1. Judgmental, attributing undo responsibility
2. Pointedly charging, reproachful
3. Condemning, censuring
4. Critical, culpable, guilting
5. Lacking praise, hard to compliment
6. Arrogant focus on self or others
7. Rejection of goodness
8. Ridicule of others or self
9. Sarcastic and emotionally biting
10. Trapped in condescending emotions

The compulsion of Gratitude is <u>submissiveness</u>.

1. Excessive beholding to others for your very presence
2. Excessive willingness to serve another
3. Abnormal devotion in an obsequiousness manner
4. Servile and fawning
5. Apologetic in atonement for vague feelings of inadequacy
6. Passive aggression
7. Sense of inferiority
8. Over-compliance to a giver's wishes
9. Chronic and excessive feelings of indebtedness, needing to repay
10. Devoid of any healthy self-esteem

---<<<>>>---

Depression
Mary's Dilemma

Mary loves to cook. She spends lots of time in her kitchen. Yet neither her teenage children nor her workaholic husband appreciate Mary's efforts and cooking competencies. She finds herself alone in her kitchen much of the time. While she experiences an underlying loneliness of heart and spirit, she nonetheless has grown accustomed to her solitary lifestyle.

Mary has struggled with the shadow of <u>submissiveness</u> for as long as she can remember. Even as a young girl she recalls her mother wondering aloud about Mary's 'over-sensitivity,' as she called it. In reality, Mary suffered from depression from her early years, and is still demonized by depression today. Mary feels unworthy, of little personal value. Even in the face of mountains of achievement and productivity, Mary persists in berating herself as insufficient. She believes that her husband only married her because he felt sorry for her. In her mind, even her children only tolerate her. She simply feels inferior. As a consequence, Mary acts in over-compliant ways with an attitude of excessive beholding to her husband, and just about everyone else for even putting-up with her!

Mary is becoming increasing avoidant of social interaction. She sequesters herself in her home, a place where she feels safe from the potential criticisms and judgments of others. Yet, Mary is her own worst critic. Her feelings are ones of self-<u>blame</u> and personal condemnation. She is irrepressively prejudicial against herself. Self-critical, and almost arrogant in her self-ridicule, Mary perpetuates her sense of personal fragmentation with the avalanches of personal rejection she heaps on herself.

Mary's gift of gratitude is all but submerged in the sea of toxin created from her intense self-<u>blaming</u> and ubiquitous <u>submissiveness</u>. While she can intellectually understand that she actually is gifted in many ways, this realization has not yet percolated down from her mind to her heart where she could affectively 'own' it as uniquely hers. She's beginning to question if God has forgotten her; she feels abandoned, forlorn, alienated, and so sad. Yet, she has not grasped that these feelings are simply the consequence of her failure to find and express true <u>gratitude</u> of heart. Living in <u>gratitude</u> means that we find joy in life because we have been so abundantly gifted. In <u>gratitude</u> we live 'in praise' of God's goodness to us. Mary is currently blocked by her shadow of self-<u>blaming</u>, and compulsion of <u>submissiveness</u> from freely expressing her profound thankfulness. Mary's depression may have biological and even chemical roots, but it clearly finds its ongoing energy in her inability to express her innate loveableness ... her submerged spiritual strength of <u>gratitude</u>.

Chapter Thirteen
Personality Function Five: Deciding

How your personality makes decisions

It's been said that life is a series of decisions, decisions, and more decisions. Making decisions is not an option if you want to live fully, yet making decisions can be perplexing. Every success and every failure begins with a decision.

Personal Power: Change, Strength, & Empowerment

Healthy change requires strength, and strength is derived from personal power. All change, especially change required for healing and spiritual deepening, requires an attitude of "charting our own course," or self-empowerment, of being able to influence events, and being resourceful. Change demands self-control and self-discipline, all ingredients of the deciding function of your personality. Decisions ensure that positive change actually becomes a working reality in your life.

Personal power is often misunderstood. It's easy to think of personal power in an absolute sense – that we either have personal power or we don't. In reality, we all have personal power; the question is to what degree have we tapped into our own personal power by making prudent choices ... making decisions?

Self- Confidence

Increased self-confidence emerges as a by-product of deciding with personal power. Some individuals who are ill report feeling that their self-confidence is eroding. Self-confidence has two parts: 1) valuing yourself as an increasingly integrated individual capable of using your strengths with clarity, and 2) finding the necessary resources to move from your weaknesses over to your spiritual strengths. Self-confidence is not a part of personal power; rather self-confidence arises from personal power as a consequence of making decisions.

In order to truly know your spiritual strengths you need to come to an equal realization of your shadows and compulsions, and the changing patterns, opportunities, and challenges that living with illness offers you every day. You need to challenge yourself to dig deeper into your potentials for personal power. Change is both the challenge and the catalyst for personal power development.

When you recognize your shadows and compulsions, which lie in the recesses of your personality, you reach a fuller, more integrated expression of your own personal power ... your ability to make decisions. Somewhere in your developmental path you are confronted with the inevitable truth that you can neither hide from, nor cover over your shadows and compulsions, neither defend nor conquer them; neither fix them nor rehabilitate them. Your shadows and compulsions are your own; you must come to own them. In doing so you find a new personal power heretofore unrecognized and unappreciated – the power of inner peace and patient resolve.

It's in the personality deciding function where you make your decisions, the choices that determine the quality of your life.

Did you ever stop and think about all the decisions you make in a single day? You make decisions like, when to get out of bed, what to wear, whether to exercise, what food to put in your mouth, how to get to work, the mood you'll take into work, your productivity, the words you use, the general attitude you'll project, the way you interpret what happens to you, your evaluations about others, the very feelings you let linger in you, and on and on. Your world can be conceived of as a classroom of choice where you make decisions that ultimately help you, and you also do the opposite ... we all do.

Who or what is in charge of your deciding function, or what we might call your free will? This takes us back to the true self and the false self. Decisions made in and through your personality deciding strength are choices grounded in universal love, while decisions driven by either your deciding shadow or compulsion force you to make choices out of fear. This is a stark dichotomy, but as you become more aware of the decisions you're making, and the power you have over your decisions, you'll quite naturally begin favoring choices motivated by your true self. Such a process is a slow one, but one that eventually transforms all your personality functioning as well as yourself. You turn over your personality to your true strengths and away from the ego protectionism or ego inflation that makes you unhappy. If your ego is directing you, then you're not self-directed.

What are decisions?

You live by your decisions, yet most of us are unaware of how we make our decisions, both the little, everyday ones, and the huge life-turning ones. Consider that every time you develop a strategy, how to go about some action, you're making a decision. All of your preferences are decisions, as well as your goals, your life objectives or life purpose, any options you develop, plans you make, priorities you rank, and of course the choices you choose are all decisions. When you act with volition, you have raised a decision to the level of commitment. Have you ever made any New Year's resolutions? Have you adopted a new course of action? Have you determined a better alternative? Have you embraced a life philosophy, a political party, a community, a new job or career; are you or have you ever been married or divorced? These, too, are all decisions. Have you taken a stand, picked a winner, selected a piece of candy (or any food), committed to a cause, or insisted upon something? Again, these are all decisions; decisions you can stick with or change at any time.

In my counseling practice, I find it so striking often times after I've investigated the full breadth of one of my counseling patients lives, I attempt to frame a question that moves us forward. I might ask something like, *"Well, now that we've clarified your life a bit better, what options do you see for yourself now?"*

What startles me every time is when they look at me incredulously, as if to say, *"Options, I have options? I don't see any options for me now!"*

When this happens I always ask, *"Who's making this decision that you have no options; is it your true self, choosing from your personality strength, or your false self, favoring fear?"*

Personal Choice is a Choice

The personal empowerment necessary for making choices begins in the believing function of the personality where we develop a conception of ourselves as a person who is allowed to make personal decisions or not. We give ourselves permission to act on our own volition, or we don't! This is one of the premier goals of counseling, and a standard requirement for living a full life: do you give yourself permission to make decisions or not? Again, who is in charge of your deciding function, your true self or your false self? Do you make decisions from your strengths or from your fears? The answer to this question is the tipping point between a full, rich, free, and satisfying life, and one of servitude.

Deepak Chopra says that we are the sum total of the decisions we make, and of course not making a decision is also a decision, albeit an unconscious one. Dr. Jane Regan, a professor at Boston College say it this way, *"Persons who have developed this discipline (personal decision making) have a clear sense of naming what matters most in their lives and recognizing the core integrity of their lives."* (p. 122, Toward an Adult Church)

Decisions are inescapable, yet we invent creative ways to avoid them. We push them away with whatever means we can conjure up; we procrastinate, we simple forget (repress) them, we neglect them, we deny them, we give them to someone else, we let time make the decision, or we let a crisis develop that removes the decision from our shoulders.

Some of us want to avoid decisions so badly that we try to put our lives on automatic pilot. There's lots of ways to do this. We become legalistic, relying too heavily on rules and regulations. We raise suggested or standard operating procedures to the level of 'must' and 'should' and 'have to.' We regiment our daily life to the level of habituation and enter into what I call a 'rote' life style; we live today just like we lived out yesterday. We can start sleepwalking through life, not really awake to the possibilities and potentials for fuller living available to us. We become frozen in our own indecision; we impulsively dart away to diversions, and entertainment, and coping strategies of all kinds to fill the void. That piece of cake or dish of ice cream works very well to fill us; the TV is an excellent tool for scheduling our lives, and then there's the video games ... before you know it you've eaten up another two or three hours, all 'directed' by your false self.

Another trick we play on ourselves is investing in the illusion that it's possible to live life without making decisions; it's possible to just stand still, marking time. Without decisions, our life falls out of sync with our true self. Our plan for happiness, expressing our gifts and demonstrating our strengths that define us, all lay fallow in our psycho-spiritual basement. Consequently, our personal life script remains unspoken; our unique symphony remains unplayed. We walk through our life in a chronic sadness, feeling separated and abandoned. Our false self can't seem to stop wresting decision-making control away from our true self. So how do we take that control back?

Continuous Decisions

Whether you're aware of it of not, you are constantly making decisions. Healing and spiritual deepening require that you first make the decision to become more aware of your decision-making behaviors and patterns. Being able to step back and recognize where and how you're making decisions, and the impact your decisions are having in your life, is step number one in raising the level, or the quality of your decision-making. And what makes for a quality decision? The answer is simple.

> *A quality decision is one that is powered by the energy of your deciding spiritual strength.*

The corollary to this is that the quality of your decisions drops as you move away from your deciding spiritual strength and move toward either your deciding shadow or your deciding compulsion. But before you can take this step, you need first to look at the underlying decision you're making all the time.

The following decisions are ones that you make almost unconsciously; you don't even know that you've made these decisions, but you have. Review these decisions and ask yourself how you are answering these basic, underlying decisions everyday of your life.

Ten Underlying Spiritual Decisions

You are continuously choosing between ...

1. The Spirit or the world. The Holy Spirit, God's power moving in the world, is constantly nudging you to

perceive God's truth, beauty, and goodness as they find demonstration and fulfillment in your life. The world instructs you to find fear, while the Spirit instructs you to find love.

2. <u>Wakefulness or sleep</u>. Are you awake to the fact that you are making decisions, or are you to some degree asleep? Are you awake to the voice you're listening to the most in your decisions: the voice of your spiritual strength, or the voices of your shadow or compulsion? Your ego speaks to you through the voices of the shadow and compulsion. These voices speak of competition and winning, of self-interest and self-indulgence, of power and personal fame, and of fortune and control. The voice of your spiritual strength speaks of cooperation and sharing, of connection and fulfillment, of energy and humility, and of true treasures and acceptance.

3. <u>Forgiveness or condemnation</u>. Forgiveness removes that which stands between you and others. Forgiveness opens up the lines of communication between you, and others, and God so you can see the true reality. Condemnation attacks others and precludes your release from the bondage of the ego desires. How aware are you of the choices that you're making between these two every day?

4. <u>Peace or turmoil</u>. Your inheritance is peace. Your spiritual strengths rest on a foundation of peace. Peace is only from God, and you are from God. The world teaches the opposite, it teaches turmoil through your shadows and compulsions. Which are you choosing?

5. <u>Freedom or confinement</u>. Where does freedom come

from, the shadows and compulsions, or from your spiritual strengths? Grace, in the form of spiritual energy, offers the highest form of freedom, freedom from worry and anxiety. All that flows from fear confines the soul, while all that flows from love offers ultimate freedom.

6. Unity or separation. There is no separation on the spiritual level. We all share in the endowment of our spiritual strengths; we all spring from the same source. You are never separated from your source, even though you may feel detached and even forlorn at times. These sensations only spring from your shadows and compulsion. Unity, peace, and harmony come only from God, and only to you through your spiritual strengths.

7. Meaning or meaninglessness. Without the realization of the presence of Spirit in us we live in a meaningless world – a spinning carousel of nonsense. You become aware of your purpose in life through your spiritual strengths working to animate your personality.

8. Truth or error. Truth is part of the living water offered to us by God. This water offers eternal life. When we choose truth, we are choosing life, and receive peace as a by-product. Truth cannot be described or explained, it can only be experienced.

9. Being happy or being "right". This is the favorite expression of Dr. Jerry Jampolsky, author of *Love is Letting Go of Fear*. He asks, "Would you rather be right or happy?" Being happy means choosing to let God share in your decisions. The world needs to be right, which is why it is characterized by criticism. Anger and

condemnation are emotions that separate people, while forgiveness is the function that can make you happy.

10. <u>Internal or external</u>. When you decide that your life is the life of Spirit, then you are choosing God's path … the healing path. When you focus exclusively on that which is outside of you and outside of the true interests of your sisters and brothers then you are choosing with the world. Inside you can rest in sanity with your Holy Self, while outside there is insanity … unreality. Have you learned yet to choose from the inside out, not from the outside in?

Chapter Fourteen

The Five Spiritual Strengths,
Shadows, and Compulsions
of the Deciding Function of the Personality

Here are the five spiritual strengths of the deciding function of the personality, along with their corresponding shadows and compulsions. One of these strengths is your premier strength, the guiding strength of your deciding function. You identified your premier deciding strength when you took the *Spiritual Strengths Finder*. Of course, you're also most vulnerable to the shadow and compulsion that stand as foreboding anti-energies on either side of your premier strength.

Compulsions<<<<<<<STRENGTHS>>>>>>Shadows

indecision <<<<<<<<< **Harmony** >>>>>>> chaos

unresponsiveness <<< **Patience** >>>>>>> impulsiveness

brutishness <<<<<<<<<**Strength** >>>>>>> impotence

unreality <<<<<<<<<**Transcendence** >>>> worldliness

self-repression <<<< **Self Discipline** >>> self-indulgence

21. Harmony is …

- Live in accordance with a central principle
- Exist in unified calmness and develop a consistent whole
- Be 'in sync' with universal love
- Live in accord with the central principles of the cosmos
- Build a personal symmetry with love
- Celebrate in unison and perfect alignment with peace

The shadow of Harmony is <u>chaos</u>

1. Disorder, internal shambles
2. Disorganization, abyss, void
3. Lack of agreement, strife, dissonance
4. Conflict, contention, dissension
5. Difference, variance, quarrelsome
6. Personal fragmentation
7. Lose moral sense of humanity and wholeness
8. Separations from self, others, and God
9. Lack clarity of mind
10. Personal confusion and/or inner turmoil

The compulsion of Harmony is <u>indecision</u>

1. Paralyzed by doubt
2. Endless hesitation in deciding what is "right"
3. Reluctance for clear-headed consideration
4. Over-heated conscientiousness of discernment
5. Excessive rumination over one's decisions
6. Endless hesitancy trying to decide "what's right"

7. Headlong direction to "keep options open"
8. Trying to please everyone
9. Fear of making the wrong decision
10. Scrupulosity, perfectionistic

---<<<>>>---

Career Fragmentation
Marsha's Avoidance

indecision <<<<<<< Harmony >>>>>>> chaos

It happened again, Marsha was asked to see her supervisor at the end of the workday. She knew what was coming; she was about to be fired. Marsha was familiar with this ritual; she had experienced it many times before. Her work history was a checkered pattern of fits and starts, getting a new job only to lose it several months later. At first Marsha blamed her supervisor and the organization, but in time she turned her anger against herself and slipped into a psychological posture of avoidance. Eventually she became tired, she didn't want to work for fear of failure, but she felt like a failure because she wasn't working. This conundrum took hold of her and contorted into depression, an emotional weight that held her back and gave rise to even deeper avoidance.

Marsha's life spiraled into chaos; she became confused and personally disorganized; her personal integrity, her sense of wholeness had eroded away. The further she moved away from her last job the more she pushed to return somewhere – anywhere. But her succession of terminations followed her and confounded her job search efforts. She was wracked with indecision, which rendered her unable to move forward. Yet, she was so unhappy in her "stuck" position. She was paralyzed with self-doubt, hemmed-in by fear, and psychologically sabotaged by indecision. She wanted so badly to move forward but each time she tried, she was too easily overwhelmed by the potential for failure that she simply wanted to give-up.

Marsha's occupational problem was rooted in her desire to please. She desperately wanted to please her supervisors, indeed; Marsha wanted to please everyone. Marsha would become so determined to doing well that she became perfectionistic, and distorted herself into turmoil. Marsha berated herself unmercifully. Without anyone ever knowing it she brutally beat herself for even a hint of imperfection. Her supervisors became concerned about Marsha not because she was incompetent, not at all! What alerted her supervisors was Marsha's anxiety, her uptight presentations, and shaky demeanor. Marsha was prone to crying and actually criticizing herself under her breadth. When a supervisor would point this out to Marsha, she would misinterpret the supervisor's remarks as criticism and reflexively react in a less than professional way. More than once these reactions alone targeted Marsha for termination.

Gradually Marsha began to find her spiritual strength of harmony. She recognized her own self-sabotaging patterns at work and, with the help of a coach, began to get a firmer grip on herself. She steadied her emotions with clearer thoughts centered on harmony. She actively tried to align her decisions with loving principles and in so doing was able to quell her "fight or flight" reflex considerably. Marsha started experiencing the calming effects of peace and a new sense of life balance. She began to invite <u>harmony</u> into her life; she lived <u>harmony</u>, breathed it in, let it saturate her, and found in her efforts a new beginning for her life.

22. Patience is ...

- Tap into the mysterious calm of the universe
- Calmly continue in the face of adversity or hardship
- Transcend worldly impulses and replace them with the surety of love
- Transform irritability and annoyance into peace
- Replace the frantic excitement of the world with universal light
- Ascend to the still point of ultimate tranquility

The shadow of Patience is <u>impulsiveness</u>

1. Demanding action NOW
2. Explosion, attack, punish
3. Impel, elbow, drive
4. Spontaneous, impetuous, compulsion
5. Sudden, thoughtless decision, reaction
6. Overly spontaneous, seeing no options
7. Impetuous decision-making
8. Sudden and thoughtless reactions
9. No deliberation, no considerations of choices
10. Hastiness, inability to wait

The compulsion of Patience is <u>unresponsiveness</u>

1. Extortion of one's personal motive power
2. Listless, sluggish, doltish

3. Over-vigilance against anything that may disrupt lifestyle
4. Indolence of decision
5. Sleepwalking...unconscious refusal to look at options.
6. Decidedly insensitive to others needs
7. Refusal to disrupt personal 'comfort zone'
8. Turning off your personal switch
9. Fear of making mistakes
10. Lack of receptivity to overtures from others

---<<<>>>---

Alcoholism
Ingrid's Co-dependency

It was 11:30 pm and Ingrid's husband Martin still wasn't home. This meant that Martin was either at the bar, or he hadn't yet left his office where he kept a private liquor supply. In either case Martin was drinking and most probably drunk. Ingrid's heart began to race as it always did when she fell into her pattern of feeling simultaneously worried and enraged. The questions began flying through her mind: *"Why does he have to drink?"* *"Why doesn't he care more about me and the children?"* *"Doesn't he know he could kill someone driving drunk?* On and on the questions swirled, as her anger grew exponentially.

Her first impulse was to call him, yet she knew exactly how the conversation would go. She wouldn't be able to control her temper. She would demand that he return home immediately. She would follow this with a stampede of thoughtless reactions that would only push Martin further and cause him to react in kind. He would "punish" her by not coming home at all. For the next three or four days only silence would pass between them, a silence that was like torture for Ingrid. Ingrid had lived this scenario many times. She knew she didn't want this again, but she was without direction or plan.

Martin's blatant <u>unresponsiveness</u> to her emotional needs made Ingrid react likewise. She avoided him, wouldn't give him eye contact, talked to him through the children, actually slept in one of the kid's bedrooms, and didn't prepare meals for him. Ingrid essentially "turned off" to Martin; she existed as though he didn't exist. Yet all her seeming <u>unresponsiveness</u> screamed that she wanted action from Martin. Ingrid wanted Martin to stop drinking, and she wanted it now! The current condition of their marriage was not what she had "signed on for." She saw no options other than Martin becoming sober. This thought consumed her, and pushed her to live a life completely defined by her reactions to Martin's alcohol dependency.

Through what could only have been an act of God, Ingrid found Alanon. This proved to be her lifesaver. In Alanon she learned she was relating to Martin's alcoholism not from her deciding spiritual strength of <u>patience</u>, but only from the shadow of <u>impulsiveness</u> and the compulsion of <u>unresponsiveness</u>. Ingrid learned that she didn't have to "fix" Martin, and that she did have a marriage even with Martin actively drinking. She learned to tap into the eternal peace of <u>patience</u> that existed in her and move away from her shadows and compulsions. She learned to center herself; her choice for centering was prayer. As she learned to replace her frantic attempts to change reality she was able to discover a new personal tranquility. In time, Ingrid became the full spiritual adult that was always inside her, but not expressed. Martin gradually recognized his need for sobriety and eventually joined AA.

23. Strength is …

- Be a potent change agent for self and others
- Resist attack with vigor
- Know that you cannot be spiritually hurt in any way
- Be straightforward and upright in action
- Have the capacity for sustained exertion

The shadow of Strength is <u>impotence</u>

1. Powerless, weakness
2. Lacking in vigor or power
3. Lack of self-trust
4. Overcome by doubt, fearing taking a stand
5. Overpower personal determination and volition
6. Powerlessness, inability, incapable
7. Incompetent, unendowded, crippled
8. Disabled, paralyzed, rudderless
9. Exhausted, shattered, demoralized
10. Weak, lacking vigor and/or power

The compulsion of Strength is <u>brutishness</u>

-

1. Decisions not considered, reasoned choices

2. Lack of rational sense and order to decisions
3. Forced, violent, and stupid choice making
4. Base, insensible, and inarticulate
5. Impelled to quick, indelicate discernment
6. No real discernment
7. Impelled to quick, indelicate choices
8. A twisted pride of self
9. Denial of personal brokenness
10. Prone to reactive, and heavy-handed decisions

Personal Pain
Rhonda's Strength over Tragedy

It was 2:38 am and Rhonda couldn't sleep. She cried into her pillow as she lamented the events of the day. Today she was fired from a job she grew to love over the past ten years. It was her perfect job; she worked with people, had lots of creative latitude, was affirmed by all, and on top of all this, she was well paid. She couldn't have asked for more. But a new supervisor, asserting her control, had somehow targeted Rhonda as a means of demonstrating her new power. When Rhonda was informed of her termination, she had but 30 minutes to vacate the premises. She was not only flabbergasted by the fact that she was fired, but she was filled with incredulity at the way she was fired. Now, only hours later, Rhonda was mentally enumerating all the ways her life would change. She was broken!

Rhonda felt powerless, <u>impotent</u>, and full of self-doubt. She was shattered, nothing like this had ever happened before.

Somehow she gathered herself and within the week Rhonda was "pounding the pavement' looking for a new job. She reactively took a job she thought would be temporary but what happened next was the 'perfect storm' that unraveled her life.

Rhonda was a single mom, and in one week her 17-year-old son was arrested for drunk driving, her ex-husband stopped child support payments, her house was struck by lightning and burned, and her sister was diagnosed with terminal cancer. Rhonda's almost perfect life collapsed like a puppet whose strings had just been severed. She emotionally sank like a rock; she couldn't work and so lost her new job. She exhausted her slim savings legally defending her son, trying to make up for lost wages, finding new housing, and buoying up her sister. It took only six quick months before she was advised to file for personal bankruptcy. Physically exhausted, emotionally devastated, and spiritually demoralized by her fall from respectable living, she felt utterly impotent.

Rhonda decided that her way out of her mess was gambling. She forced a choice that certainly was reactive, senseless, and simply stupid. She lost the small amount of money she borrowed from a friend right there on the casino floor.

Driving back from the casino that night she began to reclaim her life. She visited a healing coach who helped Rhonda find her inner gift of strength. Gradually, Rhonda became for herself the constructive change-agent she'd always been for others. She gathered herself up in her strength, reassembled her former vigor, resisted temptation to play the victim role, and regained her capacity for action. She would not fail, she would not fall, she would survive – her inner gift of strength gave her new resolve, new direction, and new motivation. Rhonda would be OK!

24. Transcendence is ...

- To go beyond the material dimension of 'doing' to the dimension of 'being'
- Growing from the worldly level to the spiritual level
- Transformation to a new paradigm
- The ability to live in the 'material' and the 'spiritual' simultaneously
- Being fundamental changed, converted, dramatically altered
- A core shift to true and higher reality

The shadow of transcendence is <u>worldliness</u>

1. Finding what's wrong, fault-finding
2. Blind to intangible concepts of truth
3. Prone to condemnation, gossip
4. Find it easy to attack others
5. Dazzled by the sparkling tinsel of the world
6. Models personal turmoil and contradiction
7. Living in darkness, easily jealous
8. Seeking one's "salvation" in the world
9. Excessively individualistic, ego-centric
10. Living in fear, covets neighbor's things

The compulsion of transcendence is <u>unreality</u>

1. Lack of rational sense and order to decisions
2. Decisions made in the realm of fantasy

3. Prone to vague daydreams
4. Failing to see Love in reality
5. Failing to see personal boundaries
6. Inflated, expansive personal expectations
7. Blind to truth in discernment
8. Lost in reverie
9. Easily off the point
10. Lost in own "world"

Prostate Cancer
Dick's Submerged Competitiveness

Dick pulled himself out of bed as the alarm sounded. At 4:30 am the winter world was dark as Dick pushed toward his desk. Dick wanted to finish writing his next book and the early morning was the only quiet time he could wrest from his schedule. As department chair in a medium sized university, Dick had expanded every aspect of the department's operation – more students, more grants, more inter-collegiate committee memberships, more teaching, more public speaking, more mentoring, and certainly more and more articles and books. Dick's department had become a veritable conveyor belt of productivity, with Dick turning the crank ever faster.

It wasn't that Dick was contorted by personal ambition; he had no desire to become president of the university, or even dean of the college, but Dick simply couldn't turn away from an opportunity. And Dick saw opportunity everywhere. His creative mind saw no end to the possibilities in his field; there were so many mountains to discover and climb. Dick could see them plainly and wanted to climb them all.

Little cracks starting appearing in his normally controlled life. He increased his office hours, called more meetings, sat on more doctoral committees, and applied for more grants. On and on the juggernaut rolled. Dick's one evening drink became two and sometimes three, he stung more than one faculty member with his irritability, he cut corners in his writing and teaching, he spent less time with his family, his sleep became restless, and he wondered where all this frenetic activity was going. And yet he couldn't stop himself. His life morphed into an <u>unreality</u> of achievement. Reading a book or a journal article sparked new ideas that Dick couldn't get out of his head until he brought them into reality. Every idea seemed a siren song calling him to action. Without being aware of it at all, Dick had sunk into the quicksand of <u>worldliness</u>. He was hooked by the possibilities for achievement and success that the world offered. Dick became dependent on success, it became his drug-of-choice, everything he did and all with whom he interacted he enlisted into his unreal worldly compulsion for 'more."

At Dick's yearly medical physical, his family physician remarked that he didn't like that Dick's PSA has jumped. "*Just to be on the safe side I'd like you to see a urologist,*" said his physician. The urologist moved quickly to a prostate biopsy. It was like a kick to the stomach when Dick got the phone call from the urologist, "*Dick, you have prostate cancer.*" It took this news to sufficiently shake Dick into a new reality. He had been living a fantasy, and unrealistic level of work unbalanced by leisure had distorted his life and perverted his soul. He had to turn his life around, but how could he?

Dick took a week-long retreat and extended it to two weeks. He clarified how he had molded his life into something unsustainable, something unreal. He needed to tap into his true strength, and what he found was his premier spiritual strength of <u>transcendence</u>. *"It seemed so easy,"* he thought. He needed to de-construct the 'somebody' he had become, and reconstruct a new identity based not on *doing* but on *being*. <u>Transcendence</u> transported him beyond his world to another, a realm where achievement isn't measured by worldly productivity, but by the simplicity of being in love. <u>Transcendence</u> moved Dick to love, and away from the fear that had originally compelled him to strive, strive, and strive some more for worldly success.

25. Self Discipline is …

- Enforcing obedience from one part of yourself onto another
- Molding your own character in the direction of your spiritual strengths
- Imposing order upon yourself
- Adopting supremacy of your spiritual (true) self as your primary goal
- Developing in ways unattainable before

The shadow of Self-Discipline is <u>self-indulgence</u>

1. Laziness, idleness, inactivity
2. Inertia, slow, sluggish
3. No self-control, unfettered, expressing no governance
4. Pandering to lowest self urges

5. No order, lacking self-obedience, or will-power
6. Lack of self-control
7. Consuming beyond satiation
8. Enticement for personal success – dreams
9. Over doing anything
10. Compelled to excess

The compulsion of Self-Discipline is <u>self-repression</u>

1. Spirit crushing personal restraint
2. Free-will contorting demands on self
3. Giving "shoulds" of life over-control of self
4. Excessively holding down desires
5. Heavy-handed suppression of normal desires
6. Imposing stricture rather than deciding on structure
7. Suppression of normal and even healthy desires
8. To push away normal wants
9. Stoically ignoring pain
10. Imposing abnormally harsh self-control

---<<<>>>---

Internet Addiction
Sam's Conundrum

Sam looked at his clock, 3 am; he'd been at his computer since 10 pm. What had he accomplished in five hours? Yes, after months of effort, he's achieved grand champion status on his favorite Internet game, *Demons & Damsels*, but what of it? How did this help him, his wife, or his three children? How did this help his new business? He told himself that he was doing marketing research, but that never happened. His gaming had taken over his life.

In times past Sam showed exceptional self-discipline. In high school he was president of the student body and captain of the swim team. In college he was a debate team standout. In his first job he was slated for the fast track of success. All this seemed a lifetime ago, a time when Sam was "on top of his game," when he know how to create order in his life. All of his former self-discipline, however, had eroded in a sloppy self-indulgence ever since he left his job and went out on his own.

He started his new business in a flurry of excitement and resolve. For the first three months it seemed he barely even slept. He lost weight, was essentially estranged from his family due to overwork. In a rush to find quick success he had imposed an overly strict time frame for various benchmarks of accomplishment. He suppressed all his usual outlets, and gave his life over to a torrent of "should" thoughts that all but tormented his countenance. Sam drove himself like a perpetual motion machine and relentlessly pushed himself with a cascade of <u>self-repressive</u> demands.

Now, Sam had reversed himself. His self-repression had "morphed" into self-indulgence. He was emotionally flat, mentally dull, disinterested, avoidant, and generally indifferent. His computer game became his means of some artificial personal accomplishment. Sam seemed bereft of any semblance of self-control; he had become lazy and prone to idleness; he fettered away his time with abandon. His computer was his only enticement. Sam was addicted, and he knew it, but he seemed helpless to move beyond it.

One morning, after only four hours of sleep, his phone rang. It was his old boss asking how Sam was faring in his new business. His boss sensed the flatness in Sam's voice and inquired whether Sam had any interest in returning to his old job with the company. Sam's heart raced as he considered the offer.

One hour later Sam called him back to accept the position. The new job seemed to rejuvenate Sam; it resuscitated his old self-discipline. He established goals, created personal schedules, adopted a new attitude, and developed a new resolve of success. A week later Sam realized that he hadn't played one computer game since he accepted his new position; self-discipline had reappeared in Sam's life once more.

Chapter Fifteen
The Acting Function of Your Personality
What you actually do

"Jesus doesn't ask us to be successful, only faithful."
Blessed Mother Theresa of Calcutta

All of creation, all that we can see, and the utter vastness of what we can't see, is the result of the action of a powerful hand. The elegantly swirling galaxies, the incomprehensible distance of space, the vibrancy and tenderness of the star nurseries, the terrible power of black holes, and the dazzle of the seas of stars, all bespeak a wonder of divine action so gigantic as to far surpass the tiny limits of the human mind. All of this action is the result of energetic hand acting at and from the source of all power, a benevolent hand of purpose – the hand of God.

Actions move things, and hearts, and minds, and souls. Actions cause change, a condition innate to the universe. We change as a result of action. Often times this action of personal change is unperceivable in the material world; change is only experienced from within. The change of conversion is deep yet the casual observer can't recognize it until she looks with newly opened eyes upon an interior landscape so dramatically rearranged as to show no resemblance to its former terrain.

While some action is outward, most is inward. The world cannot see the interior changes in believing, or perceiving, or thinking, or feeling, or deciding; no, the world can only see the exterior change in our behavior, our acting function. Yet, as the carpenter from Nazareth reminded us, *"My kingdom is not of this world."* My reading of this passage brings me to many thoughts and new conceptions of truth, but perhaps most of all it brings me to the fact that this Spirit of God acts most decisively in the bosom of my interior.

Our Life Cause

Author and personal motivator Anthony Robbins says that an action is a cause set in motion. Living optimally requires that we have a life cause that is bigger than ourselves. Philosopher Viktor Frankel reminds us that life without a cause becomes a meaningless succession of triviality. Too many of us suffer the illness of living a life devoid of cause. A cause is interior; it begins as a seed in your believing function, for a cause is something or someone you believe in. This cause, when activated by your believing strength, stimulates your perceiving strength to search your environment, both interior and exterior, to find whatever will help animate your cause. The result of your new perception, in turn, awakens your thinking function strength into developing new meaning of all this, which stimulates your feeling function spiritual strength to generate feelings that will further enhance your cause. You search your deciding function where your unique spiritual strength energizes you to come up with goals, objectives, options, strategies, and a final decision of how your cause can be set in motion. This decision motivates your acting function spiritual strength to initiate change and inspire people so your cause can move toward reality.

Yet, the cause, the action you wish to set in motion, may not be visible. Suppose you wish to change your general attitude because you notice you're becoming somewhat negative in your perception and interaction with others. You activate your believing function strength, usually by prayer, contemplation, writing, sharing, or otherwise turning it over in your mind, to modify your attitudes (beliefs) about the focus of your desired change.

Prayer as Action

Prayer is a powerful marshalling agent of spiritual energy. Prayer focuses you, centers you, and brings you to the true power of your personality. Prayer can spell the difference between personal growth and stagnation, energizing development and lifeless inertia, and between spiritual vibrancy and a shallow emptiness. Prayer sustains us because it makes us connect with the source of our true strength, which we need to rely on in order to align ourselves more harmoniously with the nudging of the Spirit. When embraced in earnest, prayer gives our lives a depth perspective and direction we otherwise wouldn't have. Prayer inspires us because it deepens our communion with the source of all power; it heightens our capacity for truly aligning ourselves with our spiritual strengths.

One of my favorite prayers is what I call the "Personality Prayer" because it addresses all six functions of the personality.

God is …

> the source of
> my belief,
> the eyes with
> which I see,
> the mind with
> which I think,
> the heart in
> which I feel,
> the will with
> which I choose,
> and the
> strength in
> which I act.

Whether your particular brokenness is physical, emotional, psychological, or spiritual, prayer offers you a primary means of healing. Your brokenness can bring you to your knees both literally and figuratively; it can make you feel helpless. And yet, your brokenness can become your spiritual curriculum by teaching you how to relate to and with your spiritual strengths more meaningfully. It's not the fact of our brokenness that brings us closer to our true spiritual strengths; rather, it's the way we respond to our brokenness that offers the means and power to become more who we truly are. Richard Rohr, author, teacher and Catholic Franciscan priest says it this way; … *in our brokenness we find our blessedness.* Here we find an essential, core understanding of our entire spiritual strengths model.

Without our brokenness, our shadows and compulsions, we could never appreciate the grandeur of our blessedness, our spiritual strengths. This is a profound insight that casts off so much of the guilt that so many of us feel as a consequence of our offensive infractions or ominous omissions. Our "sins," actions of commission and omission, are manifestations of our shadows and compulsions. While these are noxious and disdainful in themselves, when these infractions are seen as the absence of our strengths, our shadows, or as the distortion of our strengths, our compulsions, we can see that while detestable in themselves, these infractions always point to the blessedness in us, our spiritual strengths. Without our spiritual strengths we could never suffer our shadows and compulsions.

In his book *Healing Words,* Dr. Larry Dossey, M.D. writes that prayer can guide and sustain us so we can courageously confront our trials. Prayer is a primary tool for addressing the fear and anxiety that generally accompany sickness, especially protracted sickness. Prayer can vitalize us, so that the severity of our ailments seems to lessen considerably. Prayer takes many forms. Perhaps the most widely used form of prayer is prayer of petition, where we seek a specific outcome. When we ask God for a cure to our affliction, a remedy for our maladies, or a cessation to our pain, we are engaging in petitionary prayer. Dr. Dossey points out that prayer of petition can be rather presumptuous on our part. We, in effect, tell God what to do.

Dr. Dossey contrasts this with what he calls prayerfulness. *"Prayerfulness is accepting without being passive, is grateful without giving up. It is more willing to stand in the mystery, to tolerate ambiguity and the unknown. It honors the rightness of whatever happens, even cancer."* (page 24) This form of prayer

– this state of being in prayer – is what Dr. Dossey seems to favor in his work. *"Prayerfulness allows us to reach a plane of experience where illness (and sickness) can be experienced as a natural part of life, and where its acceptance transcends passivity. If the disease disappears, we are grateful; if it remains, that too is reason for gratitude."* (page 27)

 Dr. Dossey tackles a persistently knotty question that always emerges when prayer of healing is discussed: is there a special formula, some universal form, type, or sequence of prayer that will "work" for all persons? Dossey's response – having reviewed hundreds of medical research projects – is clearly in the negative. He states that our prayer needs to be as genuine and personal as possible. He advocates renewing our personal commitment to God by focusing on gratitude for God's love, and combining that with a deep acceptance – not to be confused with submission or resignation – of God's will, regardless of the outcome. He claims that those who receive healing through prayer do not follow some regulated formula or strict sequence. They do not engage in a mindless, heartless, and soulless rote method of prayer. They pray with their whole being from the uniqueness of heart and soul. Dossey writes: "Get well formulae that advocate spiritual practices are by definition inauthentic because they require that one take on spirituality from the outside, instead of allowing it to emerge form the center of one's being." (page 32)

Every Cause Requires Action

Every cause requires action; indeed many a failure is spawned by inaction. Our central life cause calls us to action, and sometimes, if not most times, the call to action is at least uncomfortable for us. Too many calls to action go unanswered causing disastrous personal turmoil and pain. In Scripture, the rich man refused his call to action from Jesus, and we're told that he walked away sad. And where do we walk to as a consequence of our own inaction? Many of us walk away to diversion and entertainment that flows unendingly in our culture. We walk to denial and submission, to resignation and doubt, we walk away to idle busyness and ceaseless striving for "more," all of which makes us sadder. We may make the decision to take action, but the decision lacks commitment and the action is stillborn, leaving us perplexed at ourselves and blaming the world. Every cause requires action.

What blocks us from taking the action, from the leap of faith required for every personal goal to become reality? Do we lack the talent, or the resources? Not hardly! We have talent and resources in abundance. What we lack is the passion to raise our acting gift, our personality acting function strength, to an operative level so it can work the real magic and mystery of God's way in our life. And what robs our passion? Fear gets in the way, fear in many forms, but most significantly the fears in our shadows and the consequences of our fears – our compulsions. Our essential separation from God introduced fear into our hearts. We wanted to be like God and took the 'forbidden fruit' only to discover our false self, the ego who promises everything and delivers nothing. This impostor, this manipulator is our ego, our false or unholy self. Our ego false self insists that only it can save us from the chaos of the world; and since we know the world is in chaos, the ego has a rather easy 'sell.' So in desperation and driven by fear we capitulate to the siren song of our false self. When we do this we simultaneously forfeit the power of our acting function spiritual

213

strength, and fall instead into our acting function shadow and/or our compulsion. There's no real energy in either of these, so the life cause we want to set in motion, the life call we'd like to achieve, remains unanimated, no energy goes toward it. As a consequence, we too walk away sad.

Creative Acceptance: the ultimate action

Creative acceptance, and its many variants, gives us the strongest means to overcome the tragedy of passionless existence. Creative acceptance is not passivity, it's not submission, and it's not resignation. Creative acceptance is what I like to call true spiritual grit in that it bounds over our ego pleadings and leadings and bring us to the doorstep of the power invested in us by the Holy One. Creative acceptance is receptive only to God's leanings, and says 'no' to everything else.

Creative acceptance means truly 'owning' your heritage as a child fro the Holy One, genuinely embracing your love-energies, your unique spiritual personality power. Creative acceptance means remembering you are not first and foremost a physical entity having a spiritual experience, rather your are essentially and fundamentally a spiritual entity having a physical experience here on this earth. You are not a body; you are body, mind, and spirit in a classroom called life learning the curriculum of true reality called Love. Creative acceptance means taking on love and loving as your only goal, a kind of overarching super-goal that transcends all else making all other goals merely secondary bit players on your stage of life.

Letting-go as Premier Action

Creative acceptance also means letting-go. Letting-go, suffering the loss, is the highest form of detachment from the desires of the ego, the finest expression of self-abandonment, giving your True Self the executive power of your personality, and the grandest form of self-surrender, relinquishing the remote control of your life to the Spirit.

Letting-go means giving-up vainly trying to control and letting people and things simply be. Letting-go means giving-up predetermined outcomes and living the mystery of life. Letting-go means stepping-up to the plate of your own life and hitting the home run of not blaming. Letting-go means letting others be themselves and not trying to change them. Letting-go means living in the 'now,' not in the guilty past or the fearful future. Letting-go means dedicating your life to loving, i.e., living in your spiritual strengths.

Action vs. Reaction

How often do we allow the world, i.e., forces outside of our own volition, to dictate our actions? How frequently do we let others direct our lives? When we do this we are not performing actions, rather we are simply reacting without truly engaging our unique spiritual strengths. Often it's not easy to determine whether we're acting genuinely or fraudulently reacting. Here are several distinguishing factors that may illuminate the distinctions:

Actors are balanced, they are 'in command' of their own actions, whereas reactors seem to be in a perpetual state of frenetic imbalance and subordination.

Actors are self-starters; they initiate action. Reactors are considered 'other starters' never taking the initiative themselves.

Actors are acutely aware of their external surroundings and their internal topography. Reactors seem to fall asleep at the wheel of their lives.

Actors act on purpose and with direction, while reactors seem vague and directionless.

Actors are quite independent of worldly trends, fads, and styles. Reactors can be fearful and vulnerable to what everybody else is doing.

Actors live an *arrow* lifestyle, while reactors live a 'pinball' lifestyle.

Actors seek responsibility. Reactors shun responsibility.

 The golden rule calls us to love our neighbors as ourselves, and to do unto others what we would have them do unto us. The golden rule does not say believe unto others, or perceive unto others, or think, feel, or decide unto others; no, it's clear that we are to do (act) unto others. We do unto others best through our giftedness; indeed, the spiritual quality of our actions rests on the thoroughness with which we use our acting function spiritual strength in our 'doing.'

Forgiveness as Action

Perhaps the highest form of creative acceptance is the action of forgiveness. Every religious tradition extols the necessity of forgiveness; this is especially true of Christianity. Yet, forgiveness is misunderstood, which may explain why so many people can ignore, deny, or otherwise distort forgiveness. So, what is forgiveness? To understand what forgiveness is, we first need to enumerate what forgiveness is not. Forgiveness is not being soft or wishy-washy. Forgiveness is not forgetting, as in 'forgive and forget.' Forgiveness is not excusing, not letting someone 'off the hook,' not forsaking someone, not pious righteousness, not even reconciliation. You don't have to become friends with the person you forgive, you don't even have to like them.

Forgiveness is first giving up our claim to recompense. When someone wrongs us, or does us harm, forgiveness allows us to hold them accountable, to pay for damages, but forgiveness does not give us permission to extract anything beyond that. We take no liberty to make the offending person grovel or even apologize, even though an apology would be appreciated. Next, forgiveness means we look beyond the error of the action to the motivation of the person, judging him/her not by worldly justice alone but also by the mercy of divine justice. Next, we try to remove our ego from the interaction. Our ego always wants retribution, wants to win, always seeks something for itself, it even wants to take advantage of the offender. There is no room in true forgiveness for any of this. Forgiveness in its highest form, means coming to the realization that the horror of the infraction that we thought took place, really didn't happen! This is an extremely hard concept to get our minds around, but it essentially means that even though this infraction may look like an attack upon your personally, it wasn't an attack in the sense that it lacked motivation. All actions are motivated by something or someone. The motivation for these actions may appear completely illogical to us, and yet, at the time it made sense, however imperfectly or crudely, to the perpetrator   here is the ultimate spiritual action – forgiveness.

The person we most needs to forgive is usually ourselves. Yet this forgiveness may be the hardest action for us because self-forgiveness requires us to change our personality, an action the ego regards as a violation of self. Yet, true forgiveness of self necessarily means shifting some long-held beliefs we have of ourselves; it means reshaping our perceptions, retooling our thinking, resculpting our feelings, and it requires entirely news decisions. All of this rearranging is focused on the most granite-like sentinel of the personality – our ego.

Action Words

There are so many words in the English language that describe action, probably because Western culture is so action (doing) oriented, rather than 'being' oriented. In any event, some words that may help us better understand the acting function of the personality include the following:

Rules of behavior

Failures and successes

Responses and reactions

Performance and achievement

Work and operations

Progress and accomplishments

Putting one's best foot forward

Buckling down

Being vs. doing

Taking charge

Taking the initiative

Taking a risk

Walking your talk

Following through

The Serenity Prayer: a model for action

All action of course is not effective, often times we allow our actions to be entirely directed by our ego. When this happens our actions can be misdirected, haphazard, confused, non-specific, perfectionistic, unorganized, or lacking in passion. We need some guidelines to assist us in determining not only what action might be required but also whether the proposed action is appropriate. The Serenity Prayer, used as a philosophical basis of all 12-Step programs (including AA and it's derivatives), is an excellent example of a model for contemplative action. The prayer provides a template for assessing the quality and appropriateness of any particular action.

The graphic below breaks down the components of the Serenity Prayer and gives us a new vision for action.

	Can Be Influenced	*Cannot Be Influenced*
Take Action	Mastery	Ceaseless Striving
Do Not Take Action	Giving - Up	Creative Acceptance

Chapter Sixteen

The Five Spiritual Strengths, Shadows, and Compulsions of the Acting Functions of the Personality

Here are the five spiritual strengths of the acting function of the personality, along with their corresponding shadows and compulsions. One of these strengths is your premier strength, the guiding strength of your acting function. You identified your premier acting strength when you took the *Spiritual Strengths Finder*. Of course, you're also most vulnerable to the shadow and compulsion that stand as foreboding anti-energies on either side of your premier strength.

Compulsions <<<<<< STRENGTHS >>>>>> Shadows

skepticism <<<<<<<<< **Truth** >>>>>>>>>> deceit

excitability <<<<<<<<< **Inspiration** >>>>>> lifelessness

co-dependency <<<<<<<<< **Kindness** >>>>>>>> indifference

arrogance <<<<<<<<<<< **Courage** >>>>>>>>> timidity

imperilousness <<<<<<<<< **Perseverance** >>>>>>>>>> giving-up

26. Truth is …

- Being fair, sincere, and true to the primary fact of divinity
- Having elevated honor and integrity
- Freedom from internal fraud and deception
- Letting the petty and/or trivial go to unclutter one's life
- Going beyond worldly honesty and entering divine honesty

The shadow of Truth is deceit …

1. Being fraudulent, either to others or to self
2. Trying to trick, cheat, or fake self or others
3. Advancing untruth
4. Manipulating the truth
5. Misled by 'white lies'
6. To give false witness
7. To be cunning
8. To bluff, or circumvent the truth
9. To swindle, cheat, or fake
10. To perpetrate a hoax

The compulsion of Truth is skepticism …

1. Taking on a mindset of repetitious critical questioning
2. Fearful of gullibility, self-conscious of feeling foolish
3. To doubt or excessively question
4. Finding it hard to believe – incredulous
5. Developing a critical attitude
6. Image conscious
7. Believing in no absolutes – agnostic

8. Suspending judgment
9. Withholding comment
10. Disposition of incredulity

---<<<>>>---

Alcohol Abuse
Steve's Distrust

skepticism <<<<<<<<< **Truth** >>>>>>>>> deceit

Steve slammed his hammer on the floor breaking several floor tiles and cursing his inability to do the job right. It was taking Steve longer and longer to complete his work as a home remodeling specialist. He had plenty of work to do, but his depreciating self-talk was robbing his initiative and making Steve increasingly <u>skeptical</u> that he could ever again become the energetic, efficient worker he once had been.

 Steve didn't know when it happened but he only recently noticed his escalating critical attitude. His thinking became skewed toward disbelief in himself and in others. Steve was becoming singularly <u>skeptical</u>. He questioned himself, he questioned his work, he questioned his friends and family, he questioned just about everything. Those big existential questions; *"Who am I?" "Where am I going in life?" "What's my life been all about all these years?* all swirled around him like a swarm of bees. Steve had always been a bit self-conscious, even as a young boy in school he felt anxiety about being called on by the teacher. He was a good athlete in high school, but he was afraid of his coaches' criticism; he was chronically afraid of making a mistake and being ridiculed. Lately however, his anxiety level had skyrocketed well beyond anything he had ever experienced.

Steve not only doubted himself, he doubted others as well. Little things upset him, an inaccurate weather or traffic report, the evening news, any mistakes that he or someone else made, would raise his ire. He found so much of his life simply incredulous, and constantly doubted that he could trust anyone or anything.

After months of torment and dismally low personal productivity, Steve finally consulted a healing coach. He quickly discovered that he suffered a grave disappointment and even betrayal early in life. Steve was one of four children and in sixth grade when his brother, two years his senior, contracted a life threatening disease. For the next two years the family was swept up in a medical care maelstrom that sucked their time, attention, and in Steve's perception, their affection away from all else but their gravely sick son. Just when Steve was crossing the developmental bridge to <u>trust</u>, the rug was proverbially pulled from under him. Without realizing it Steve emotionally imploded into himself. He cut others out of his life and learned to rely only on himself. His protective self-trust and doubt of all others escalated dramatically. Unable to trust, he was unsuccessful in forming intimate relationships. Steve had many acquaintances, and many dates, but could never develop a true friendship, or a long-term love relationship. He found solace only in work and alcohol.

Steve began AA, and with his healing coach's steadying influence, he came to a clearer understanding of the mammoth walls he had erected to protect himself from rejection, betrayal, and ridicule. Steve credits God working through his AA group for the gradual dawning of <u>trust</u> back into his life. It was a hard and emotionally treacherous hike for Steve, but he did manage to pullout of the darkness of <u>skepticism</u> and personal <u>deceit,</u> and into the light of <u>trust</u>.

27. Inspiration is ...

- To be infused with light and life
- Motivated by the brilliance of celestial reality
- Touching the spiritual reality within you
- To acknowledge the mighty mechanisms of care and healing deep within you
- To recognize Love's healing power and strength to work wonders in your life

The shadow of Inspiration is lifelessness ...

1. Being deadened
2. Having no vigor
3. Lack of spirit
4. Dampened spirit
5. Impervious, vapid, lack luster
6. Threatened and timid
7. Sleepy, unaware
8. Putting life actions 'on hold'
9. Avoidant and passive
10. Dependent upon others

The compulsion of Inspiration is excitability ...

1. Frenetic and sometimes desperate need for stimulation

2. Nervousness, anxiousness
3. Excessive disquietude
4. Perpetual vigilance and scanning for more stimulation
5. Agitation, inflammation of spirit
6. Always 'on call,' never letting one's guard down
7. Inability to relax
8. Easily and quickly aroused to anxiety
9. Excessively sensitive to stimulation
10. Dislike of peace and harmony

---<<<>>>---

Lifeless Marriage
Sarah's Inspired Action

excitability <<<<<<<<< **Inspiration** >>>>>> lifelessness

Sarah glanced at her watch as she left work and headed for the expressway home. She was tired; she'd worked hard for the last ten hours and just wanted to rest. She picked-up her son at the day care center and braced herself the rest of the way home dreading her husband's reaction to her being late, if only by 15 minutes.

Sarah enjoyed work; she liked the quick, and sometimes frenetic pace. Sarah liked being excited, feeling continuously stimulated. She liked being "on call" and "in the loop." She was an energetic, action-oriented, and self-starting individual. She'd been called a "firecracker," and "ball of fire," and an "energy generator." All these gave testimony to her need for constant movement, constant <u>excitement</u>. If something wasn't happening, Sarah would make sure that it did. Sarah was compulsive, but no one seemed to mind. She was perky, always with a smile, a giggle, a light word; she brought gaiety whenever she went, everywhere that is except in her own home.

Sarah's believed that her husband was the polar opposite from her. Where she was energetic and ambitious at work, to her he seemed passive and taciturn. Sarah was "all smiles" and he was all frowns, pouts, and bluster. He reacted against her effervescence, he seemed to resent it. Her husband was the only person that Sarah couldn't "win over" with her bubbly personality. It seemed like he was her counter-weight; she moved one way and he reacted against her by moving the opposite way. This was the story of their marriage.

Over time Sarah became more and more weary. She alternately tried to change her husband, and tried to accept his personality. Nothing worked for her! His apparent negativity had the effect of dampening her every joy, her every delight. Sarah began living two lives. Her home life became emotionally flat, a study in the shadow of <u>lifelessness</u>. All other parts of her life, her job, her relationships with friends and extended family, were the mirror image of <u>lifelessness</u>; it was a life of <u>inspiration</u>. Sarah breathed in the joy of life when she was outside her home; she reveled in the company of others, and experienced deep gratitude, appreciation, thankfulness, and love. Outside her marriage she felt free to breathe deeply and fully, to take in the full measure of God's wonder, while in her home she felt confined, her breathing was shallow and constrained, she existed in an emotional prison; at home, Sarah was <u>lifeless</u>.

Sarah's life groaned on without much change until the day when her husband announced that she had better change or he would move out. It seemed that he had had enough of her lifelessness. He had made this threat before but not with the conviction that she sensed this time. Sarah didn't sleep that night pondering her decision. As the morning sun gradually brought light to her dark world, she made the inspired decision that this time she wouldn't try to stop him, but instead sought help for herself from a counselor.

28. Kindness is ...

- Demonstrating gentle, affectionate, and loving behaviors
- Accepting your body as a gift from the divine
- Being tender, mild, friendly, and helpful
- Giving care
- Acting with courteous gesture and goodwill

The shadow of Kindness is neglect ...

1. Giving little or no attention
2. Disregard that which requires attention
3. Lacking in respect for basic needs
4. Not 'carrying one's weight' in groups
5. Ignoring, stonewalling, isolation
6. Arriving habitually late
7. Rudeness – acting destructively
8. Making hurtful comments – speaking severely
9. Disrespect for individual differences
10. Exhibiting little or no, heartfelt caring action

The compulsion of Kindness is co-dependency

1. Giving one's entire self in service of another's dependency
2. Over-functioning in relationships
3. Excessive solicitousness
4. Enabling addictive behavior in others
5. Smothering another with sentiment
6. Participation in cliques
7. Inappropriate prolonged flirtations
8. Subjugation of one's own needs
9. Harming self in deference to another's wants
10. Extremely loyal, even in the face that the loyalty is undeserved

---<<<>>>---

Repressed Anger
Janet's Co-Dependency

co-dependency <<<<<<<<< **Kindness** >>>>>>> neglect

Janet arrived at work late again. She withstood the stares of all the people she supervised as she strode past all their cubicles heading toward her corner office. Janet was responsible to a fault and hated being late, but her daughter was acting-out again and Janet wanted to calm her before she drove her to school. It seemed that Janet was always dealing with something regarding her daughter. Only in 10th grade, her daughter seemed to have adult problems. But Janet was determined to give her daughter every advantage. Ever since Janet and her ex-husband divorced four years ago, Janet felt sorry for her daughter. Janet was continually trying to make-up for the loss. Janet lived through her daughter to the point of becoming <u>co-dependent</u> on her daughter's chronic acting out.

Janet's almost exclusive focus on her daughter left her very little energy to devote to herself. As <u>kind</u> as Janet was to her daughter, and indeed to everyone, she was markedly unkind and even <u>neglectful</u> to her own emotional needs. Janet was unaware of her <u>neglectful</u> and certainly unconscious to how it might be hurting her. She repressed her ever-expanding anger as much as she could, but wondered to herself why she was becoming so "short" at work. She became uncharacteristically disorganized, she was misplacing things, and forgetting important facts and appointments. In the last month she had to apologize to two separate workers because she had made hurtful comments to them. Her <u>neglect</u> of her own needs due to an advancing <u>co-dependency</u> on her daughter's problems was causing Janet some real dilemmas.

Then came the day when Janet received a call fro her daughter's school principal informing her that marijuana was found in her daughter's locker. Janet began to spiral into new levels of <u>co-dependency</u>. She escalated her self-criticism, felt down and insecure, became reclusive and submissive at work, completely lost touch with herself, and made excuse after excuse for her daughter.

Janet finally consulted a counselor for herself. The counselor immediately spotted Janet's excessive <u>co-dependency</u> and commenced a therapy that allowed Janet to see how she was

230

overlooking her own needs. Gradually Janet realized how unkind she had been to herself and started a conscious self-regulating program to regain a sense of <u>kindness</u> toward herself. As Janet reclaimed her sense of self, she started becoming empathetic and compassionate to herself. As she reinstated her adulthood, Janet's daughter gradually emerged from her emotional bleakness and could once again address her life with renewed health and emotional stability.

29. Courage is ...

- Mental and moral strength to venture forth in the face of danger
- Firmness of mind and will
- Engrained capacity for meeting strain or stress with fortitude and resilience
- To hold one's own against opposition, interference, or temptation
- Determination of character to achieve one's goals
- Tenacity of a bulldog
- Resolute, bold, heroic
- Confident, fortitude, spunk
- Stand against, inspire, encourage
- Hardy, dauntless, unflinching

The shadow of Courage is timidity ...

1. Lacking in self-confidence, boldness, or determination
2. Faint of heart, pessimistic
3. Cowering, avoiding, 'turning tail'
4. Fearful, cowardly, shrinking

5. Frightened, afraid
6. Retreat, sidestep, quit
7. Evade, elude, dodge, shy away from
8. Inaction, equivocation
9. Walking out on, back away from
10. Head in the sand

The compulsion of Courage is arrogance …

1. Condescending attitude
2. Over-bearing and heavy-handed
3. Presumptuous claims of potency
4. Sense of superiority
5. Undue haste, lack of deliberation, cautionless
6. False front of power
7. Cocky, jaunty
8. Imprudent, careless, headlong action
9. Air of superiority
10. Acting with hubris

---<<<>>>---

Brain Cancer
Bill's Conversion

arrogance <<<<<<<<<<< **Courage** >>>>>>>>> timidity

He walked into my counseling office, the slight concave depression on the left side of his forehead told a story – either this man was in a terrible accident, or he had extensive brain surgery. The man was tall, about 6'4", lean, and although a bit thin, his frame was solid and his gaze was clear and strong. Bill was 38; when he was 35 he was on top of the world. He owned and ran a very successful company with 250 employees. He had a beautiful wife and two perfect kids. Bill lived in the biggest house in town, and drove the most expensive car. Bill had everything; he even still held athletic records from the state university.

One day Bill noticed an uncharacteristic headache. It intensified, and three days later his doctor referred him for an MRI of the head. There it was, a mass growing in his brain! A biopsy would identify the cancer as a most virulent type that had a 95% mortality rate after five years.

Now, three years later, Bill needed to tell his full story, not the story of his sickness, but his story of conversion and healing. His eyes drove into mine when he said, *"I thank God that I have cancer."* *"Bill, what makes you say that?"* I asked. *"Because I was living a stupid life before I had cancer. I thought life was about worldly success, now I know differently."* Bill went on to describe his experience. What followed was a hallowed story of pure <u>courage</u>. Bill faced death with a mental and moral strength I'd rarely, if ever seen. *"I was scared and so was my wife, but God told me to be resolute ... God made me a puppy dog, but the puppy was a bull dog."*

Bill had been through it all, two huge surgeries at MD Anderson in Houston, new diet, and new exercises. His business failed and he had to sell the big house. Nonetheless, Bill entered every new traditional medical and non-traditional therapy he could, always with the faith of <u>courage</u> lifting him up. <u>Timidity</u> would invade his psyche at times, but he pushed it out. *"God* *emboldened my spirit and brought me through the times of trial. I kept thinking of the <u>arrogant</u> life I lived before cancer. I always took everything for granted, and appreciated nothing."* Bill explained how he had inherited the family business, how athletics and studies came easily to him, and how he had an <u>arrogant</u> sense of entitlement about life. All that changed with struggle.

At first his confidence dropped, he tried to avoid the whole thing, and he even had thoughts about ending it all in an acts of <u>timid</u> and <u>arrogant</u> desperation. But as he ventured into the bowels of fear, after he cowered in the easy way out, he felt shaken back to the base of himself and there he discovered a stalwart strength, a new capacity to not only ride out the storm, but to see the turmoil as a new path for living differently.

Bill was healing, and even if the cancer were to take him, he had touched the divine reality within him, he had rallied around the stanchion of spiritual strength that best defined him and held him up – he had tasted the fullness of his spiritual strength of <u>courage</u>.

30. Perseverance is …

- Persistently plodding in your cause, mission, or personal purpose
- Possessing singleness of purpose, tenacity
- Proceeding when others would have lost hope
- Running the extra mile, and the extra mile, and the extra mile
- Having stamina, backbone, and spiritual grit

- Staying focused on the light of love even when your spirit is dim
- Commitment beyond the ego wants

The shadow of perseverance is <u>resignation or giving-up</u>

1. Surrender or terminate prematurely
2. 'Throw in the towel,' to withdraw
3. Surrender, desist, avert from
4. Declare insoluble when solutions do exist
5. Despair, withdrawal from activity
6. Yield, bring activity to an end
7. Terminate, become exhausted
8. Submit without sufficient cause
9. Buckle under weak pressure
10. Retreat with inadequate provocation

The compulsion of perseverance is <u>imperilousness</u>

1. Endangering self or others unnecessarily
2. Placing oneself in path of danger or destruction
3. Putting oneself in unnecessary jeopardy
4. Excessive risk to life, limb, treasure, family, etc.
5. Action without regard for caution, propriety or danger
6. Putting oneself in peril in body, mind, or spirit
7. March into 'death,' or 'go down with the ship'
8. Failure to respect safety
9. Unnecessarily "playing with fire"
10. Getting "in harms way" without defensible cause

---<<<>>>---

Marriage Troubles

Philip and Marcy's Excessiveness

imperilousness <<<<<<<< **Perseverance** >>>>>>>>> giving-up

Philip reached for his pen to itemize all the ways that his wife Marcy has "wronged" him in the last week. This has become a habit for Philip in the last year, as his relationship with Marcy seemed to falter. Philip's mind traps every potential slight, or omission, or supposed disregard or disrespect that his ever sensitive emotional 'radar' picks up. He assembles all these transgressions of Marcy's and calls a Sunday evening session to 'process' them.

 Philip's compulsion of <u>imperilousness</u> always orchestrates these meetings to proceed along a predictable path. Marcy reluctantly 'comes to the table' and listens as Philip reads his list following each item with rationalized embellishments. Marcy silently stares at her husband during this recitation with a look of contempt pasted on her face and a desire to run away. Once finished, Philip stares back at Marcy wanting a reaction from her. The mutual stare-down is usually broken by Philip who flails his arms in sweeping motions as he asserts something on the theme of, *"This is what always happens. Don't you have any reaction to what I'm saying? I care about this marriage and your lack of reaction proves that you don't!"* This blast is like a firebomb that ignites the interaction and inevitably turns it into a protracted argument. The content of the argument is ostensibly over who cares more about the success of the marriage, while in reality the argument is about who will have control of the relationship ... who will have the 'upper hand.'

As the argument escalates, each tosses in references to the shadow of giving up. *"Well, if that's the way you feel I guess there's no hope for us."* Or *"Why don't you just move out."* Or *"Maybe we shouldn't have married in the first place."* Sometimes their words are like arrows aimed to do maximum damage, at other times they plead with one another to become more of what each other wants them to be. The argument is decidedly self-centered; neither Philip nor Marcy has reached beyond their ego wants to begin thinking about the long-term needs as a loving couple. Neither has genuinely considered the true meaning of the six essentials of a spiritual relationship: togetherness, respect, communication, intimacy, trust and commitment. (Loving for a Lifetime, R. P. Johnson, 2004)

Their healing comes gradually as they tire of their attempts to change the other. The couple moves more to the center of their mutual spiritual strength of perseverance; Marcy moves away from her former tendency to give-up on the marriage, and Phillip does the same with his imperilousness and bullying. They begin thinking as a unit, and tenaciously considering their mutual interests with one another. Finally they reach the relationship pedestal of perseverance, realizing that it's OK for couples to move in and out of romantic love, and still be firmly living 'in love,' and that their mutual goal is to help the other express their unique spiritual strengths. Here is their healing.

Part Three

The Dynamics of Healing

Now that you have all the "basics" or mechanics of the Spiritual Strengths Healing Method, it's time to briefly look a little deeper into the dynamics of the Method. The three chapters in Part Three give but a taste of how the Spiritual Strengths Healing Method can be used to bring healing and spiritual deepening in many ways.

Chapter Seventeen

Dynamics of Your Healing Personality

Personality Interrelationships

Your personality is multi-dimensional, it doesn't operate from a singular perspective; it doesn't function on only one level, one strength - shadow – compulsion dynamic at a time. Rather, your personality is constantly using all six personality functions, all six spiritual strengths, shadows, and compulsions simultaneously. When you appreciate this dynamic quality of your personality you automatically gain a clearer understanding of your personality operation and focus in on a sharper vision of your healing.

Over our life course we develop, or fall into, personality patterns or habits. Some of these habits are constructive, while others are not. Constructive habits are driven by our spiritual strengths; destructive habits are driven by shadows and compulsions. Let me use my own personality (since I know it best) as an example to demonstrate some of the dynamics of personality. Here are my strengths, shadows, and compulsions:

Personality Function	Personality Compulsions	Spiritual Strengths		Personality Shadows
Believing	presumption ...	HOPE	...	despair
Perceiving	bluntedness ...	SIMPLICITY	...	complexity
Thinking	perfectionism ...	WISDOM	...	inadequacy
Feeling	ingratiating ...	EMPATHY	...	obtuseness
Deciding	unreality ...	TRANSCENDENCE	...	worldliness
Acting	arrogance ...	COURAGE	...	timidity

Believing

Looking first at my believing function, we find the strength of hope, the shadow of despair, and the compulsion of presumption. I can't say that I have ever entered into abject hopelessness, or dismal despair, but I do find myself stumbling through various points along the continuum from hope toward despair. My first step away from hope is usually to the bitterness of disappointment. I become disappointed in myself, and sometimes in others as well. My next step is usually toward becoming dispirited, feeling the enthusiasm of hope drain from me. This makes me more vulnerable to discouragement, when I begin to seriously question whether I'm living up to my purpose in life. On the heels of discouragement I can easily take the next step farther away from hope and fall into attacking my self-esteem. Usually these attacks take the form of internal questions centered on some illusionary personal worthlessness. From worthlessness it's only a quick, yet dramatic next step toward despair; I get depressed. At first my depression flares

242

into anger, but it generally morphs into a sullen, downcast silence that pushes me toward avoidance, a sense of personal rejection, and the need to withdraw. In such a flummoxed state it's easy for me to touch the sourness of the compulsion of hope ... presumption. In this state, all gratitude evaporates from my personality, my hopeful assurance in the unfaltering presence of God in my life erodes, and I find myself distant, and even out-of-touch with God's goodness and love. I paradoxically, and quite unconsciously, presume that I'm the center of the cosmos, and all persons and things should serve me. I take my wife's love for granted, I take my spiritual strengths for granted, my health, my abilities to perform and achieve, and my God-given talents now become my possessions, rather than God's presence in me. I can even become irascible and cantankerous, morose and discontent.

Hope is the engine of my believing core, but at everyday times and in common places I quite unintentionally walk away from my center, my true self, and over to the dark sides of my personality. Without forewarning or prior alarm, I find myself in a distorted emptiness of life space bereft of what is good, upright, and holy. When I move either toward my believing shadow or compulsion, I find myself energy-depleted and dry of spirit. In this mental-spiritual "space" I become vulnerable to the dysenergy of other shadows and compulsions as well. My beliefs and attitudes have become ill.

Perceiving

When I'm dispirited I begin to perceive my life and all that's dear to me as overly complex. In the shadow of complexity, all beauty of simplicity is taken from me. I become blunt and critical, uncaring and hurtful toward others and myself. I perceive those around me as harsh, threatening, and uncaring, or as lazy, boorish, and self-centered. I see myself in much the same light. My personal insight is distorted, and my outlook is bleak. At times like these my perception has become ill.

Thinking

In my thinking function, I wander away from <u>wisdom</u> and begin focusing on what I lack rather than on all the abundance in my life. I start thinking of myself as <u>insufficient</u> and <u>inadequate</u>. I seek remedy for this anxiety by "flying" over to the thinking compulsion of <u>perfectionism</u>. In this "space," I demand, I try to control, I push myself and I push others; I'm not satisfied, I struggle in my own arrogance to "hit home runs" or climb to the next rung of the ladder of worldly success. What's worse is that I believe that I should, and that something is wrong with me if I don't or can't. At times like these my thinking has become ill.

Feeling

God has given me an immense capacity of empathy, yet it seems that in the blink of-an-eye, I'm feeling <u>obtuse</u>. I don't care about the needs of others; I'm insensitive to their life requirements. I focus on me and only me, but only the ego parts of me! I have no <u>empathy</u>; I live in my own illusionary affective world feeling quite entitled to use others for my own self-interest. I even become <u>ingratiating</u> trying to manipulate the situation toward my singular interests and desires. At times like these my feelings have become ill.

Deciding

When my shadows and compulsions threaten my usual spiritual centeredness, the decisions I make in such a state all surround my ego's desires. My ego only sees <u>worldliness</u>, no other motivations are real, and so when I look through my ego's eyes I only see threat and fear. I patently pass over my spiritual strength of <u>transcendence</u>. I "fly" to the compulsion for relief and there I encounter my tendency toward <u>unreality</u>. My unreality takes the form of an illusion that I can, and that I'm supposed to "do it all." I begin writing plans and schemes, all beneficent ones, that will help others, but nonetheless hopelessly unrealistic for my resources of time and energy. At times like these my decisions have become ill.

Acting

I now crash into my acting function. In my formative years I remember that my parents' goal for me was to be a "good boy." Once I reached adolescence however, my parents quite generously tried to form me into their notion of a gentleman. The first requisite of a gentleman is that he is a man of his word; he is absolutely <u>courageous</u> in every way. My parents' view of the world was a place fought with unpredictability and danger. In their eyes a gentleman must stand steadfast in mental and moral strength. A gentleman must resist temptation, must be tenacious in upholding what is good, pure, and noble. A gentleman must be confident, so he can stand against a harsh world.

A gentleman cannot be <u>timid</u> of mind, or faint of heart. He cannot cower, be a quitter, or evade responsibilities. He must be a man of his word; he can't equivocate when called to serve.

Nor can a gentleman be <u>arrogant</u>; he cannot be heavy-handed (or what they called "ham-handed"). A gentleman is never a "hot dog," is never "full of himself," and certainly careless or cocky. He must be prudent, deliberate, and dauntless. A gentleman is confident; but never overly so, he is spunky, but never superior; and he is resolute but never crosses the line into hubris. A gentleman's word is his bond, if he says he will do something, he has no choice but to follow through. A gentleman avoids (fears) <u>timidity</u> in every way possible. Yet, where does this pursuit of <u>courage</u> cross the line into <u>arrogance</u>, a behavioral solidification that habituates life rather than merely regularizes it. At times like these my actions become ill. I, of course, never completely lived up to this unrealistic, even perfectionistic prescription, nor do I think they actually expected me to live up to them; they simply set a high bar, an idealistic bar to shoot for.

Personality Dynamism

It's easy to see that moving toward one shadow, or one compulsion sets us up to move toward other shadows and compulsions. When I inadvertently slide over to one shadow, for example the shadow of despair, I automatically become "primed" to likewise move over to other shadows. The same process works for my compulsions. When left unattended this process can spiral out-of-control and activate an avalanche of dysenergy. Ultimately I get mired down in a swamp where the shadows and compulsion dominate my personality. In such an energy-depleted position, I'm vulnerable to all measure of emotional, psychological, and spiritual pain – I begin to suffer from pervasive illness.

Chapter Eighteen

Your Personality as a Circle

Up to this point we've conceived of spiritual strengths, and their corresponding shadows and compulsions as a distinct points on a horizontal line. The strength is in the middle, the shadow is off to the far right, and the compulsion is off to the far left. We know that there are many points between the spiritual strength and the shadow, as well as between the spiritual strength and the compulsion. These intermediary points represent various feeling states, thoughts, or behaviors that gradually move you farther and farther away from your spiritual strength and toward either the shadow or the compulsion. The image looks something like this:

Compulsion . . . . .   STRENGTH   . . . . .   Shadow

In this conception, our most spiritually potent place is in the middle of the horizontal line, a middle ground between the negative forces of the shadow and the compulsion. As we move, or are pulled, either toward the shadow or toward the compulsion, we gradually lose the positive energy (grace) of the spiritual strength. If we continue our "journey" away from the strength, we can ultimately wind up either fully in the shadow or fully in the compulsion.

While this is a simple way of viewing the ebb and flow of spiritual energy (grace) movement in your personality, it is nonetheless misleading because it is a somewhat less than fully dynamic view of the interaction between and among these three. A more functional way of conceptualizing them might be to simply bend the horizontal line into a circle. Now our image looks something like this:

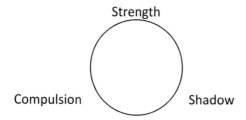

When we use this new image of personality functioning, we climb to a higher promontory point and get a clearer view of the interactions among all three. From this advantaged spot we can see that our most spiritually potent "place" is at the top of the circle where the spiritual strength resides. As we move (or are pulled) away from this summit or strength of our personality, we begin sliding either toward the shadow or toward the compulsion of the spiritual strength. This movement away from the high ground of the strength drains us of our spirit energy. If this draining continues we can eventually cross the centerline of the circle into shadow or compulsion territory.

Only rarely are we aware exactly when or how we cross the center point, or equator, of our personality and become fully "out of our strength.' There's usually no marker or warning bell to alert us that we're drifting away from our true selves; but cross the line we do.

If this dysenergy process continues unabated, either down the shadow side, the compulsion side, or some combination of the two, something quite noxious occurs ... the shadow and compulsion eventually touch. When they do, a new entity is formed. Some type of morbid synergy is created when this happens, and it sends shock waves through the personality. The personality has entered into complete dysenergy, its spiritual strength is drained and the true identity of the individual is lost; she/he becomes only a shell of their former self. The personality loses it former volition and becomes entirely directed by the outer world. If this process of complete dysenergy occurs in all six functions of the personality then the person is said to be spiritually bankrupt, there is no authentic spiritual energy (grace) left.

When completely drained, the person enters into a vortex at the bottom of the personality circle, a place where she/he endlessly swirls around and between in the shadow and the compulsion. This is spiritual confusion; we walk in darkness fearing we're going down the drain. To compensate for this confusion we can frantically latch onto some addiction: alcohol, drugs, overwork, money, sex, gambling, control, etc. In a paradoxical way this addiction provides us with the illusion of a focus, the mirage of a direction. The face shown to the world is the face of spiritual bankruptcy. Getting out of such a situation takes a miracle. This descending spiral into spiritual bankruptcy can happen to individuals, to relationships, an even to organizations. Here's a hypothetical, yet nonetheless realistic, example.

Going Down the Drain

The *International Board of Benevolence and Mercy* has 12 members. It is formed for, and charged with dispensing monies to worthy causes in the form of grants. After its inception the Board rolls along quite nicely until the time when requests for monies exceeds annual reserves. At this point the Board forms a sub-committee charged with establishing guidelines for proper submission of grant requests. The larger Board accepts the sub-committee's recommendations without dissent. The rise in grant requests continues. Two years later the sub-committee is reactivated to investigate further measures to tighten regulations for grant requests. Again the larger Board accepts the recommendations of the sub-committee. Gradually, with the best of intentions, and quite without conscious awareness, the sub-committee gathers more and more power on the Board. The Board, realizing the heightened importance of the sub-committee, even hires a consultant. More and more guidelines, regulations, and restrictions are created by the sub-committee and rubber-stamped by the Board. All the while the Board becomes more facile at denying grant requests; indeed, denial becomes the norm.

At what point does the Board cross over the line from its founding principle and guiding light of <u>mercy</u> into the compulsion of legalism? As the momentum of <u>legalism</u> gathers strength, as is the case with compulsions, legalism will eventually circle-down and meet-up with the shadow of indifference. At this point the guidelines have become so stringent that even the most deserving grant requests are denied. The Board becomes haughty and self-serving, exclusive and self-aggrandizing. The Board looks out more for its own notoriety than to help others.

The original purpose of the International Board of Mercy has been eclipsed, the Board has lost its way; it no longer operates from the strength of mercy but is now reduced into a conundrum of waffling between legalism and indifference. Eventually the Board either perishes under its own weight of dysenergy, or something of a *coup* will push out the sub-committee and try to set the Board upright again.

This little "study" of how an organization can collapse into its own shadows and compulsions is only a representative story of how our personality darkness can sabotage even our best intentions. The themes described here can be as easily ascribed to interpersonal relationships, especially of an intimate nature, as well as our interior life.

Voices

Every spiritual strength, every shadow, and every compulsion has its own voice. These voices compete as in an interior debate society. But which voices are loudest in you? Which voices sound most convincing? Which voices do you listen to the most? The voices of the shadows are shrill and fearful. The voices of the compulsions are commanding and tyrannical. The voices of your spiritual strengths are soft; they speak to you of places and powers from the depths of Truth. They are echoes of the universe, sometimes only gentle whispers; they are intriguing, even enticing, but always compelling and true. Listen deeply to the depth of your soul and you will hear the voice of God speaking to you of health and healing, of forgiveness and freedom, of truth and acceptance, all communicated to you through your spiritual strengths.

Chapter Nineteen

A Symmetry of Ideas

The ideas presented in the Spiritual Strengths Model, while novel in their construction into a comprehensive plan, are not novel ideas in themselves. Many authors over the centuries have echoed these ideas; other minds have been moved by the Holy Spirit and have expressed these ideas on personality functioning, spiritual depth, and healing in thousands of ways and places. I've read hundreds of these authors, tasted their ideas and found marvelous symmetry between and among their expressions and what God has led me to write here in this book. I've chosen three of these writers, from three different fields, with three different approaches to accent and underscore the universality of the underpinnings of the Spiritual Strengths Model. I think these quotes and the following commentary on each may further illuminate the timeliness of the Spiritual Strengths Model and make it more personal, practical, and relevant for you.

A Spiritual Solution to Our Problems

In 2001, Dr. Wayne Dyer, the well-known psychologist, author, and presenter came out with a very successful book, *There's a Spiritual Solution to Every Problem.* The book is fascinating, marvelously creative, and gutsy, in that it presents a counter-cultural alternative means for living a full life. It's a great read, especially when viewed through the eyes of healing ... I recommend it without reservation. I'd like to quote some of Dr. Dyer's insights here and place them in the context of spiritual strengths because I believe his insights are given "flesh" by the spiritual strengths paradigm described in this book.

It's in the transcendent, intangible world where we find the solution to all our problems (page 5).

What constitutes a problem for you? Is your medical diagnosis (your sickness) your problem? Or is your reaction to your diagnosis (your illness) your primary problem? Cancer, or heart disease, or kidney failure, or Hodgkin's Disease, indeed, all medical diagnoses, are certainly problematic, but they are not problems in themselves unless you make them so. When you keep your personality centered on your spiritual strengths, that which is most real about you, then the diagnosis remains only problematic and not the problem.

You will realize that every kind of disharmony, discord, or disease is amenable to the spiritual energy that is in you (page 7).

It's perhaps somewhat easier, or at least more understandable to conceive of a disharmony within oneself, like shame, or guilt, or rejection, or jealousy, and/or that a relationship discord between you and another, may find remedy in the spiritual arena, but it's a stretch for most of us to think of spiritual energy, or grace (your spiritual strengths) as the remedy for physical disease. Again, we need to draw a strict line between sickness and illness. We have the power of the medical community for dealing with sickness, but the human condition is far more pained by illness than by sickness. And what if the medical community can't find a remedy, a solution, for your sickness? What if the only "solution" is death? Is your illness a failure of sight: are you failing to perceive death as the spiritual transition that it is? Certainly we cannot blithely dismiss the loss that death presents to us, yet aren't we all called to "make peace" with death at some point? Is not this "making peace" the spiritual solution, or your personal healing?

Sense the presence of your sacred partner. You can turn you problem over to this "senior partner" and move to a place of peace (page 8).

You have a sacred partner in you, always with you, continuously nudging you back to your spiritual center ... your spiritual strengths. We call this partner your True Self, the action of the Holy Spirit within you. When you learn to consult your "sacred partner" at every step of your journey, you are already well along your healing path.

All problems are dissolvable by saturating them with the higher energy of spirit (page 9).

Your spiritual strengths are pure grace, pure sacred energy. Your goal is to continuously embrace this grace ... this strength.

Jesus said *"I am with you always,"* and so He is present in your strengths, your true healing power. This power is available to you, and is effective.

What we need is a change in our personality functioning to heal our problems. We need to rely on this power (page 19).

Your personality needs to be in a constant state of growth. When you stop growing, you become anemic and begin to atrophy, wither, unravel, and disintegrate spiritually. When this happens your healing power finds no place to work. Change is the watchword of the cosmos; everything in the universe is constantly changing. So it is with you and all of us, our personalities are drawn toward their source; all power flows out from the source, and returns to the source. God is our source!

My spiritual strengths represent my ideal, complete, union with God (page 33).

Your healing power, your spiritual development energy, all congeals in you as your spiritual strengths. This is the place of residence for 'the sacred' inside you. Here is where you come closest to God, and even touch God at times.

You created your problems; you can fix them (page 41).

Your sickness comes to you by no fault of your own, yet your illness is entirely self-inflicted … you create it.

A Cross-Cultural Perspective

In 1976, Bede Griffiths, a Catholic priest and mystic who lived the last 25 years of his life in India seeking the universal touch points between Christianity and Hinduism, wrote a book entitled *Return to the Center*. I'd like to quote from Fr. Griffiths' book and relate his observations to the spiritual strengths model.

It is only when you are free from self – that is free from self-love
and self-will, that you can really serve the world (page 13).

There's a great tension in your between your True Self (Holy
Spirit within you) and your worldly self, your ego. Your ego is
worldly in that it can only look outward to the world. Your ego
causes you to wear various masks; you can "put on" different
ones depending on the situation, or relationship of the moment.
This ego is pure self-interest, solely self-seeking. The ego
operates as if behind a veil, having no awareness of the True
Self. The ego sees threat everywhere, and therefore it "trades"
in fear. The shadows are given birth in this fear, and the
compulsions are our vain attempts to avoid the fear in the
shadows.

The great illusion is to consider that the self has an absolute
freedom, that it is law unto itself (page 14)

We say we want freedom, and so we do; yet, what is freedom?
The ego defines freedom as license to do what it wants. The
Holy Self sees ultimate freedom as freedom from ego desires
and drives. Yes, we want freedom, and we need freedom to
heal, yet what type of freedom are you pursuing? Your
shadows and compulsions are purely ego-driven; your True Self
thrives only in the freedom and truth of the spiritual strengths.

The self must either be dependent on God, the universal Law,
and acquire true freedom, or else it loses its freedom in
subjection to nature, to the unconscious (page 15).

Your personality deciding function is constantly faced with
making choices between your True Self, which only sees the
actual reality of the spiritual strengths, and your world self that

only sees its own reality, which is fear in the form of shadows and compulsions. This "reality" is but an illusion.

Redemption, 'at-one-ment' is the return to unity. The "self" is the indweller in the heart of every human. It is this Self – the indwelling Spirit – who passes from life to life (page 34).

Healing is a form of conversion, a movement away from false "reality" to true reality, a growth from darkness into light, and ultimately from death into life. Healing is sacred growth, letting go of all untruths: fear, inner pain, resistance, avoidance, denial, etc., and embracing all real truth … the spiritual strengths.

The Shadow Revisited

William A. Miller's book *Make Friends with your Shadow* gives us some insights into the dynamics of the Spiritual Strengths Model. Here is some of what William Miller has to say with commentary on how it relates to the Spiritual Strengths Method:

We move toward personality integration and wholeness, emotional symmetry and balance not by practicing moral righteousness and goodness alone, but all this must be tempered with a nod to our shadows, which paradoxically complete us (page 28).

Unbridled righteousness leads you to the poverty of compulsion -- the absence of your spiritual strength. It is folly to think that you can live in your spiritual strengths all the time. You are only rarely resting in your strengths. The fact is that while your spiritual strengths are at the center of your personality you find yourself swinging through them as though you're riding a pendulum. As you grow spiritually, the arch of your pendulum shortens, and the pace of your pendulum slows, so you naturally spend more "time" in your spiritual strengths and correspondingly less and less time in the shadows and compulsions. As your worldly pace slows, your spiritual pace quickens.

The attack of sin, remarked Martin Luther, makes the soul stronger and more temperate (page 37).

The shadows and compulsions can be most functional for your healing because they always, always point to your spiritual strengths. You couldn't have a shadow or a compulsion without first possessing the spiritual strength. Indeed, the very purpose of your shadows and compulsions is for you to become more aware of your spiritual strengths. How could you ever embrace the spiritual strength of hope, for example, if you never tasted the bitterness of discouragement, or despair? How would you know the marvelous strength of kindness without ever experiencing the shadow of neglectfulness at some level, or having "danced" with the compulsion of co-dependency?

You can learn from your shadows and compulsions; indeed, I call them the *instructive shadows* and the *illuminating compulsions*. Yes, you are to embrace your shadows and compulsions. Even though they may cause you much pain at first, they always, always point to your spiritual strengths. Your shadows and compulsions are the "back door' to your spiritual strengths. A healthy sense of inadequacy or insufficiency can save you from the arrogance of self-importance and keep you in the spiritual strength of humility, which of course is wise.

Until we walk through the valley of our shadows we will remain incomplete (page 40).

You can never completely repress your shadows and compulsions; they will be with you until the end of your days. It is only by walking with them, by even dancing with them at times, that you can learn to appreciate their value in pointing toward your holy center of truth. Your shadows and compulsions can be avenues toward peace if you regard them with the kind of respect you might give a gun or a knife. Weapons can kill, of course, but they can also protect. Your shadows and compulsions likewise can offer you useful life lessons, they deserve your intentional focus. If you use all your strength to repress your shadows and compulsions, they will soak up all that energy and only become stronger in the process. They will pick-up your disdain for them and react by having "tantrums" causing you much unnecessary pain. You need to walk through your shadows and compulsions, not ignore them.

There is a crook in every honest man (page 52).

Each of us has the capacity for evil. Evil is the intentional utilization of our shadows and/or compulsions. You've heard the adage, *"There but for the grace of God go I."* I don't know who first uttered these words, but the concept is accurate and timeless. It's only through the grace of God (your spiritual strengths) that you can successfully deal with your shadows and compulsions. Your spiritual strengths protect you from the potential viciousness the shadows and compulsions can perpetrate on others and upon you. Part of becoming whole, the goal of healing, is to open yourself to the fullness of life, not just to your spiritual strengths but to your shadows and compulsions as well. This is what it means to be spiritually receptive.

The law of opposites is personality development: the more we strive for something bright, the more its dark counterpart is babbling underneath (page 57).

The most dangerous people are those who fail to look at the potential evil inside them. When you're blind to the force of shadow and compulsion, you invite them to take over your life. When we view the tyrants of history we find men and women who allowed their shadows, and perhaps more so their compulsions, to dominate their personalities. Think of the "bad men" of history and you have discovered personalities completely off-center, personalities caught in the vortex created when shadow and compulsion merge, personalities at the bottom of their personality circle, 180 degrees opposite the power of their spiritual strengths.

Striving for perfection, thinking you must always "be in" your spiritual strengths is the surest way to push yourself out of them. Can you see the vanity of such a desire? Can you see the arrogance of believing that you have the power to conquer evil by yourself? We are all called to confront evil, yet when we approach the evil that is resident in our shadows and compulsions we need protection, we need to carry the shield of our spiritual strengths. Becoming whole means carrying our strengths high, fully aware that they will be tested.

The notion of "tragic flaw" is right under one's most potent strength (page 60).

Each of us has unique "tragic flaws." The adage *"When you live by the sword you will die by the sword."* illuminates the notion that we carry our own seeds of destruction within us. We've all read about good people who somehow fall. We've all had friends or acquaintances baffle us when their "tragic flaw" is exposed, and they plunge into a dive that ends in their spiritual death. Make no mistake that we all have tragic flaws ... our shadows and compulsions.

When you deny your shadows, you cut yourself off from the intuitive knowledge of the dark side, and set yourself up for tragedy (page 60)

Shadows and compulsions can give us an intuitive insight into others as well as ourselves. When we try to push the shadows and compulsions away we set ourselves up for a fall. Become familiar with the shadows and compulsions, learn their ways, keep them at hand, and don't lose them, because it's then when you truly walk in darkness. Always keep in your mind and heart that the value of the shadows and compulsions is that they are a reflective consequence of the spiritual strengths. The spiritual strengths are your true reality, your only true reality; your shadows and compulsions are but dialectic reflections of the strengths that only serve to underscore the reality of your True Self.

APPENDIX ONE

How to Use the Spiritual Strengths Plan

Whether you're using the Spiritual Strengths Plan for, 1) healing, or for 2) spiritual deepening, the components and sequence of the plan are identical. While I certainly see the immense value of having a Certified Spiritual Strengths Healing Coach "walk" with you through this program, I also know that you may opt to proceed through the plan on your own; that's perfectly acceptable.

Components of the Plan

1. **Spiritual Strengths Finder (SSF)**. Your first step is to take the SSF, a 120 item spiritual insight questionnaire that generates a 20 page analysis of your unique and personal, a) spiritual strengths, b) shadows, and c) compulsions, along with in-depth descriptions of how these all fit together to form your unique spiritual personality. Your SSF results constitute a spiritually magnificent document that you'll marvel at and read over and over again, each time gaining new insight into the marvelous spiritual entity that God made of you.

2. **Book:** Discover Your Spiritual Strengths. This book thoroughly describes an entirely new concept of spiritual personality. It breaks new ground by offering the results of Dr. Johnson's

research and thinking about a remarkable new healing plan, and a means to "see" your spiritual life through a dramatically broader and finer lens.

3. **The Seven-Week Spiritual Strengths Healing and Spiritual Personality Insight Program**. This seven-week program allows you an entirely new way of seeing your True Self, as well as ways of breaking through whatever barriers (shadows and compulsions) that may be blocking your healing and spiritual deepening. The program brings you step-by-step through a spiritual insight healing exercise every day for seven weeks. Each exercise is custom-built just for you, based on your unique spiritual strengths, shadows, and compulsions. You can choose to use the services of a Certified Spiritual Strengths Healing Coach, a person trained and certified to maximize the effectiveness of the Spiritual Strengths Healing Plan, to help you "walk through" this seven-week program is you choose.

4. **Book**: <u>Body, Mind, Spirit: Tapping the Healing Power Within</u>. This book contains prayers for all your spirituals strengths. There are separate prayers for morning, afternoon, and evening. These prayers are used during the entire seven-week Healing and Spiritual Personality Insight Program. They help you saturate yourself and your life with your six spiritual strengths –God's

264

grace that all flows from Love. The deeper you can move toward saturating your personality with your spiritual strengths, the more you will find yourself growing toward your spiritual center. When your personality is centered on your spiritual strengths, their power is more available for your inner healing and spiritual development.

Purpose

The purpose of the Spiritual Strengths Inner and Spiritual Personality Insight Program is quite simply to give you ...

A new avenue of approach to your God-given healing power.

A plan to harness your true inner strength, and focus this strength on whatever personal brokenness or illness that currently bedevils you.

A new vision of your spiritual personality.

A way of knowing the specific strengths that God has given to you.

An organized method to realize your full spiritual potential.

A step-wise progression to spiritual personality integration.

A means of dismantling the blocks of fear that prevent you from healing, happiness, and holiness.

A clear picture of the wonder that God has invested in you.

A deeper understanding of your True Self.

A way to identify and discard whatever "masks" you might wear that hide the "true you."

Steps to Healing

1. Take the SSF.

2. Study your SSF results.

3. Begin reading the book <u>Discover Your Spiritual Strengths.</u>

4. Order your Seven-Week Inner Healing and Spiritual Personality Insight Program.

5. Procure the book: <u>Body, Mind, Spirit.</u>

6. Decide whether you'd like the assistance of a certified healing coach.

7. Begin your seven-week program.

8. Pray each day.

You can do all this through: www.HealYourIllness.com

APPENDIX TWO

Should I Become A Certified Spiritual Strengths Healing Coach?

- If the material in this book appeals to something deep in you …

- If it touches that special "packet of divinity" within you

- If you have a call to help others in their times of need …

- If your have the vision to minister with another to help bring God's grace more fuller into their life …

…….then perhaps you'd like to consider becoming a Certified Spiritual Strengths Healing Coach.

There are lots of ways you can use a certification of Spiritual Strengths Healing Coach.

1. Naturally, you can use the materials privately, for your personal healing or spiritual deepening.

2. You can greatly up-step the work you already do as a spiritual director, chaplain, pastoral counselor, "body worker (Reiki, Healing Touch, therapeutic massage, etc.), or any other professional in the healing arts.

3. You can become, or perhaps you already are, a healing companion to someone you know who is currently dealing with a sickness, be it acute, chronic, or even terminal.

4. You can begin a healing ministry in your parish or church, your work site, or wherever.

5. You can start your own healing coach private practice in your community.

6. You can even open a Spiritual Strengths Healing School in your locale. A Spiritual Strengths Healing School can take several forms, but the basic goal of starting a Healing School is to bring your community a new way of inner healing. You can accomplish this by a combination of, 1) offering Spiritual Strengths seminars, workshops, and/or retreats, 2) offering healing coaching to individuals, and/or 3) conducting healing circle support groups. Your individual call to help others; together with your own imagination, creativity, resources, time, and energy can all be your guides in deciding whether this is for you. You can even specialize your healing practice or school. We have one coach who specializes in weight management using the Spiritual Strengths Healing Program.

The Vision

The vision of the Body, Mind, Spirit Healing Academy is to have the Spiritual Strengths Healing Method offered in every community in America and beyond, through appropriately trained and Certified Spiritual Strengths Healing Coaches. All Coaches work on their own and use the Spiritual Strengths Healing Method and resources described above, and on our website.

You can become a certified Spiritual Strengths Healing Coach by successfully completing the requirements, either through self-study, or by in-person classes. See the website for the next scheduled certification training sessions.

Contact the Body, Mind, Spirit Healing Academy for admission requirements and registration information:

www.HealYourIllness.com

ACKNOWLEDGEMENTS

So many people gave me so much help preparing this book for publication.

Let me thank the Benedictine Sisters at St. Mary's Monastery, Rock Island, IL for their grand hospitality providing me a place of retreat and respite….a place where I could organize my thoughts and put them to paper.

My thanks go to Martha Rawe who offered helpful editing suggestions in such a short time.

I'm grateful to Fran Cole, RN for her insightful and creative comments; they were a great help.

Deep thanks goes to Paul Bauermeister, Ph.D. whose adept eye and sage wisdom brought new dimension to these pages.

Finally, my deepest gratitude and love goes to my wife Sandra for her steady and continuous emotional and spiritual support throughout this writing endeavor.

R. P. Johnson